THE DELEGATION TRAP

It's Not Them, It's You

ATIBA DE SOUZA

CONTENTS

Title Page
WHISPERS FROM THE CAGE
Foreword
CHAPTER 1 - The Lies You Tell Yourself About Delegation   1
CHAPTER 2 - Why Traditional Delegation Fails   30
CHAPTER 3 - Choosing Your First C.A.S.E. Task   46
CHAPTER 4 - Why You Need An Accountability Partner (Outside Your Business)   65
CHAPTER 5 - Handing Off Your First C.A.S.E Method Task Without Losing Control   78
CHAPTER 6 - Running Your First C.A.S.E. Method Meeting—Turning Task-Takers Into Thinkers   96
CHAPTER 7 - The Art of Asking Questions That Transform Thinking   126
CHAPTER 8 - Learning From Failure—Why The C.A.S.E. Method Works Even When Things Go Wrong   154
CHAPTER 9 - Scaling Your Delegation Beyond Yourself: Training the Trainers   195
CHAPTER 10 - Let the AI Take Over (So You Don't Have To)   214
CHAPTER 11 - I Don't Answer Questions   231
CHAPTER 12 - Origins of the C.A.S.E. Method   252
CHAPTER 13 - My Mission   260
REFERENCES & FURTHER READING   273
ACKNOWLEDGEMENTS   275

WHISPERS FROM THE CAGE

Read the confessions of other leaders.

You've probably never said it out loud.
Not to your team. Not even to your partner.
But you've felt it—
That weight in your chest when you realize...
You're the one. The only one who can get things done right.
No one else cares.
You make all the sacrifices—for everyone and everything.
Late at night, other leaders—just like you—have dared to tap out the truth:

"Last week I deleted a vacation request from my calendar—because I didn't trust my team to go three days without me. I lied to my spouse and said the client changed the date."

- ANONYMOUS LEADER

"I pretend I love the grind. Truth is, I fantasize about getting the flu—just so I'd have an excuse to disappear for a week.
I've built something successful... and I secretly hate it."

- ANONYMOUS CEO

Read more Confessions

...and leave your own

FOREWORD

FOREWORD by Ryan Deiss

I've been in the business of scaling companies (and teaching others how to do the same) for over two decades. I've built teams, developed systems, and spent more time than I care to admit trying to figure out why delegation so often doesn't work the way the business books say it should.

So, when I tell you that a single framework genuinely changed the way I think about delegation, you should know I'm not one to throw that kind of praise around lightly.

That framework is Atiba's C.A.S.E. Method.

I first encountered it at a Founders Board meeting, which is the mastermind I host for growth-minded entrepreneurs. Atiba, one of our members, took the mic during a hot seat and casually dropped four questions he uses to train his team to think like owners, not order-takers.

And as he unpacked his method, I found myself leaning in and taking notes as fast and furiously as my pen would allow. Not because it was flashy. Quite the opposite. It was simple. Elegant.

And most importantly, it solved a problem that even seasoned operators like me still wrestle with: how to get your team to stop asking for direction and start showing initiative.

The truth is, I've seen delegation frameworks. I've even created a few. But C.A.S.E. Method hit differently.

It wasn't a new tool…it was a new lens…a way to bridge the gap between what's in your head and what actually gets executed.

Because if you've ever hired a "rockstar" only to find yourself still answering all the questions…

…if you've built SOPs only to find that you're still the bottleneck…

…if you've ever wondered why your team knows what to do but still can't seem to make decisions without you…

…then you're about to understand exactly why this method matters.

What Atiba has done here is remarkable. He has taken a deceptively simple idea (asking better questions and getting better thinking) and built a system around it that can scale across roles, departments, and even entire companies.

C.A.S.E. Method creates clarity.

It fosters ownership.

It's what delegation looks like when it's done right.

That's why I'm thrilled to see Atiba expanding it here, in its full form, with all the nuance, application, and real-world stories that make it such a powerful tool.

So read it. Apply it.

But more than that…use it.

Try it on one project, one teammate, one meeting.

You won't need a six-week bootcamp to see results. Just

four questions…repeated consistently.

This is the kind of thinking that separates managers from leaders, employees from owners, and burnout from freedom.

Atiba didn't just create a delegation framework. He built a system for unlocking human potential inside your business.

And if you let it, it'll unlock yours, too.

Ryan Deiss

Founder & CEO, The Scalable Company and DigitalMarketer
Author of Get Scalable - The Operating System Your Business Needs To Run and Grow Without You, Digital Marketing for Dummies (2nd Edition), and Invisible Selling Machine (2nd Edition)
Proud advocate of the C.A.S.E. Method

CHAPTER 1 - *THE LIES YOU TELL YOURSELF ABOUT DELEGATION*

"What got you here won't get you there."

—MARSHALL GOLDSMITH

Let me ask you a direct question: Are you tired?

I don't just mean physically. I'm talking about being tired in your soul. The kind of tiredness that sinks into your bones and whispers, *"Tomorrow will be exactly like today."* You'll wake up early, respond to a million messages before your first sip of coffee, and solve everyone's problems, including those that aren't even yours to solve. Maybe—*maybe*—you'll manage to squeeze in a shower between back-to-back meetings. And by the end of the day, your to-do list is longer than when you started. Sound familiar?

Somewhere along the line, you realize something painful, And yet, you keep going. You tell yourself, *"I just need to tough it out a little longer."*
You keep chasing that magical *next quarter* when everything's supposed to calm down.

But that quarter keeps getting pushed.

That tunnel? It just keeps stretching further into the distance.

I've stood in front of enough conference rooms and workshop stages to know you're not alone. I see the same weary eyes. I hear the same half-joking "I don't even remember what sleep feels like" lines. Deep down, we all know: **We've built our own cages from the very excellence and hustle we once prided ourselves on.**

But here's the shocking truth: that cage is entirely self-made.

According to a 2023 Harvard Business Review survey, the average CEO spends 61% of their time on tasks someone else could do. But only 30% of those tasks ever get delegated.

That's not a leadership strategy—that's self-sabotage.

The Cage: How We Lock Ourselves In

Entrepreneurs are masters at building things.

Unfortunately, that includes building their own **perfect prison.** The raw materials? Your beliefs about delegation. The bars are forged from statements like:

- "It's faster if I just do it myself."
- "My team just isn't capable of operating at my level."
- "I don't have time to train anyone."
- "I'll delegate later—when we're in a better place."
- "No one cares about the quality like I do."

Each one sounds logical in the moment—after all, you're a doer, you have high standards, and you can't afford a costly mistake. But these "truths" form the vertical bars of a personal cage, keeping you from scaling, resting, or even stepping away for a weekend without your phone lighting up every ten minutes.

I know this intimately because I spent years locked inside my own steel delegation trap of "only I can do this right." When I finally realized I had the keys all along, it felt like discovering hidden instructions for how to break out. And that's exactly what this book

—and The C.A.S.E. Method—is about: giving you a blueprint for dismantling the cage you've built.

But first, we have to dismantle the biggest lies keeping you stuck. Because if we don't address *those*, then no strategy—no matter how brilliant—can set you free.

Lie #1: "It's Faster If I Do It Myself"

Whenever I'm speaking at a conference, I always like to ask the audience: "Raise your hand if you've ever said, 'It's faster if I do it myself.'" Almost every hand goes up, usually with an embarrassed grin. Then I'll ask: "Now keep your hand raised if you said that more than once this week." Almost the same number of hands stay in the air, maybe with a few sheepish laughs.

That's exactly what happened at a Chamber of Commerce talk in Houston last year. After the session, a woman named **Laura**—a busy marketing agency owner—approached me. She confessed that she had a small team of talented people, yet she was still pulling midnight shifts, tweaking client proposals, rewriting ad copy, and handling "quick" design changes.

> *"It's just easier," she said. "I could teach my junior designers, but it's such a hassle. I have to review their drafts anyway. And I can do in 30 minutes what takes them three hours."*

On the surface, Laura's logic makes sense. But like so many entrepreneurs, she's too focused on the short-term "faster." She doesn't realize that while she's saving a few hours now, she's losing hundreds of hours over the long haul—plus draining her mental energy and risking burnout.

The Real Cost of this Delegation Trap

- **Burnout Over Time**: You're not a Superman. You run out of gas because you're doing it all.
- **Team Dependency**: Your team never develops the muscles needed to think and produce at your level.
- **Zero Scalability**: If you get sick, go on vacation, or shift focus to a new project, everything stalls.

Every time Laura stepped in to "fix" things, she taught her team something dangerous:

"Don't worry—I'll handle it. While the "it's faster if I do it myself" lie keeps you trapped in the day-to-day execution, there's an even deeper belief that reinforces this cage—one that has less to do with time and more to do with trust.

Lie #2: "My Team Just Isn't Capable"

I met **Ron** during a workshop for second-stage startup founders. We were chatting despite growing from 5 to 40 employees, he was still the one closing every major deal.

> *"Nobody on my team can close the way I do,"* he insisted. *"I wish I could trust them, but they don't see the angles or read the nuances. I'm the only one who can do it effectively."*

Ron believed his team lacked the innate "gift of the sale." But after we dug deeper, it turned out he'd never really shown them his approach. Sure, he'd run a few quick role-plays. He'd even created a standard pitch deck. But he never once took the time to break down the subtle questions he asked, the intangible signals he picked up on, or the improvisational way he read a client's vibe.

To his team, "Ron's magic" was just that—**pure magic**. Something they would never replicate. Because nobody gave them the slightest idea **how** to replicate it.

Why This Lie Is So Destructive

- **Self-Fulfilling Prophecy**: If you believe no one can match your caliber, you won't invest in teaching them how to do it.
- **Team Disempowerment**: Over time, employees begin to believe they really can't match your skill. So they stop trying.
- **Founder Burnout**: You remain the only "expert," guaranteeing you never escape the day-to-day grind.

Often, when a founder insists, "My team just isn't capable," they're really saying, "I don't know how to transfer my thinking and expertise." And **that's** the gap we're going to fix with The C.A.S.E. Method.

This belief that "my team just isn't capable" often walks hand-in-hand with its close cousin: the conviction that you simply don't have the bandwidth to change the situation.

Lie #3: "I Don't Have Time To Train Anyone"

This is the daily-grind version of the "time" excuse—where you're convinced every single day is already maxed out, so training is a luxury you can't afford now (or ever).

I met **Manny** at a technology conference in Austin, where he ran a successful SaaS business but was drowning in everyday operations—everything from final code reviews to frantic late-night debugging sessions.

> *"If I stop to train someone, that's hours I could be coding," Manny said, sipping his fifth coffee of the day. "And by the time they learn, I could've finished it myself."*

In his world, each day was a series of urgent tasks. He was always a few hours behind, always playing catch-up. So training felt like a "nice to have." Meanwhile, his dev team was too dependent on his approval for code merges, bug fixes, and architecture decisions—because **he'd never shown them the deeper logic behind his choices**.

The Immediate Costs of this Delegation Trap

- **Daily Firefighting**: You stay stuck as Chief Problem-Solver because your team lacks the skills they need (and that you never taught them).
- **Task Bottleneck**: The more tasks you claim for yourself, the more your to-do list grows—and the more "essential" you become.
- **Constant Interruptions**: Employees ping you all day for clarifications, approvals, or crisis fixes because they haven't been trained to solve issues on their own.

Yes, training takes time and energy. But if you refuse to invest that effort right now—even an hour a day or a few hours a week—**you guarantee that tomorrow will be more of the same**. Manny didn't lack time—he lacked the courage to invest time in empowering his team.

When the present feels too overwhelming to invest in training, the mind naturally seeks refuge in the future—creating perhaps the most seductive lie of all.

Lie #4: "I'll Delegate Later When We Have More Money/More Time"

This lie sounds similar to Lie #3, but the difference is it's a **future-oriented promise**—the idea that "one day, you'll have plenty of time and resources to do it right." Instead of confronting your daily bottlenecks head-on, you keep pushing them into an imaginary future where everything magically calms down.

Sandra is the perfect example. She was an e-commerce entrepreneur from one of my workshop Q&A sessions who kept telling me:

> *"Once we move into the new warehouse, I'll set up all our SOPs. Right now, it's just too hectic."*

Months later, they'd moved into the new warehouse, but chaos had only **grown**: more inventory, more shipping demands, bigger client orders. The "perfect moment" to delegate never came. Instead, Sandra was even busier than before.

Why This Is a Delegation Trap

- **Endless Postponement**: If you're always waiting for the "right time," you'll put off delegation indefinitely.
- **Increased Complexity**: Growth brings new levels of complexity—**not** the free time you imagine.
- **Compounded Stress**: The longer you wait, the more pressure piles on. When you finally do attempt to delegate, you're overwhelmed by everything that needs systematizing.

In reality, the best time to start delegating was **yesterday**. The second-best time is **right now**. Because if you keep waiting for ideal conditions, you'll look up in a year—or five—and realize you're still in the same cage, just with more problems.

Postponing delegation "until later" might seem like

practical planning, but it often masks a deeper, more personal barrier—one rooted in our identity as founders and our attachment to quality.

Lie #5: "No One Cares About The Quality Like I Do"

On stage, I often share a personal story from the early days of my businesses I was stuck rewriting every piece of marketing copy obsessing over every word. I'd say, "I have to do the final pass—no one else on the team cares about brand voice or detail like I do."

Let me tell you: that belief doesn't just wear you down—it actively prevents your business from developing the resilience it needs to survive without you. Because while it may be partially true that no one is as **emotionally** invested as the founder, **it can become an excuse to stay stuck**.

Barb, a solopreneur turned small-agency owner,

realized that her unstoppable drive for perfect brand experiences was crippling her design team. She'd insist on redoing mockups before they went to clients. She'd rewrite proposals "for tone." Eventually, her staff gave up trying to meet her unattainable standard, and Barb found herself working longer hours than she did as a solo freelancer.

The Delegation Trap

- **Micromanagement**: Your team sees you swoop in to "fix" everything, so they figure, "Why bother giving it my all if Barb's just going to redo it anyway?"
- **Founder Burnout**: You become a perpetual safety net, catching every detail, every nuance, every potential error. That's exhausting.
- **Blocked Team Growth**: Your employees never get the chance to level up their own judgment or creativity.

But the moment you let people try—and even fail a little—they develop genuine ownership and pride. Over time, they come to **care as much as you do**—sometimes more. That's how real high-performance cultures form.

This belief about being the sole guardian of quality completes the circle, reinforcing the first lie that "it's faster to do it yourself." Together, these five deceptions form a perfect cage—comfortable enough that you might not even realize you're trapped.

Recognizing the Cage (and That It Has a Door)

All these lies—the "I can't trust my team," "I don't have time to train," "I'll do it later," "No one cares like I do"—are the metal bars that keep you locked in. The irony? They're also your comfort zone. It's **weirdly comforting** to believe you're indispensable. To think, "I matter so much that if I let go, everything collapses."

But let me put it bluntly: If your business crumbles the moment you step away, **you don't own a business; you own an exhausting job**.

> *The cage you're in has a door—it's built right into the design. You just haven't seen it. Let me clue you in:* ***The C.A.S.E. Method*** *is that door.*

It's a simple, powerful system for turning your

intuitive genius into a teachable, repeatable process your team can follow—and even improve upon. But if you're not ready to admit you're the one holding the keys, no method (no matter how good) will help you.

Real People, Real Struggles

Before we wrap up this chapter, let me share a few short snapshots of entrepreneurs who came up to me after a keynote or workshop, desperate for solutions:

1. **Pedro, the exhausted "firefighter"**

   - **Business:** A thriving HVAC repair company.
   - **Struggle:** He'd get calls at all hours from employees unsure how to handle repairs in the field. Pedro ended up driving hours to job sites because "They can't see what I see." His teenage son joked that their minivan was "Dad's

second home."
- **Underlying Lie:** "My employees can't do the critical work as well as I can."

2. **Cassandra, the reluctant "bottleneck"**
   - **Business:** Small but successful accounting firm.
   - **Struggle:** She insisted on reviewing every client's taxes, forms, and final invoices for fear of mistakes. Tax season was a personal nightmare of 90-hour weeks. Her team quietly resented the repeated last-minute rewrites.
   - **Underlying Lie:** "If I don't double-check everything, we'll lose clients and ruin our reputation."

3. **Zach, the "I'll fix it next quarter" optimist**
   - **Business:** E-commerce brand scaling from 2 to 8 staff.
   - **Struggle:** He knew he needed better

systems but always found an excuse —inventory issues, holiday rush, launching new products. He told me (with a tired laugh), "I've been planning to set up SOPs for a year."
- **Underlying Lie:** "We'll have time once this next urgent situation is sorted out."

They each found themselves in a cage. Sometimes, you don't realize how stifling those bars are until you see how they're made.

The Risk of Staying Locked Up

If you keep repeating these lies, your cage only gets stronger. Here's the risk:

- **Business Stagnation**: You'll struggle to scale beyond a certain point because you're the gatekeeper of progress.

- **Team Turnover**: Good people don't enjoy feeling underutilized or mistrusted. They'll leave for places where they can stretch and grow.
- **Lost Opportunities**: You can't explore new ventures or strategic deals if you're always playing "Chief Everything Officer."
- **Personal Burnout**: Chronic stress, health problems, strained relationships—these come with the territory of carrying the entire load. A longitudinal study tracking founders across five years found that those who failed to implement delegation systems were 3.8 times more likely to experience significant health issues and 4.1 times more likely to report relationship problems at home.

Worst of all? You become resentful of the very dream you once cherished. That's a tragedy I don't want for you—and I'm betting you don't want it either.

The Path Forward

Good news: No matter how many times you've repeated these lies, you're still the one who holds the keys to your cage. By learning a better approach to delegation—one that actually transfers your decision-making to your team—you can build something that frees you and lifts everyone else up at the same time.

That's where The C.A.S.E. Method comes in. It's a systematic way to capture your unique genius, so you're not just giving your team tasks or SOPs—you're giving them a framework for thinking, problem-solving, and innovating.

In Chapter 2, we'll tackle why **traditional delegation** has likely failed you before—and how C.A.S.E. fixes those exact issues. But first, I want you to take one step toward opening that cage door:

ACTION STEP: Identify One "Only I Can Do This" Task

Grab your copy of the **C.A.S.E. Method Workbook** (www.TheDelegationTrap.com/workbook)

There's a place for you to jot this down clearly.

1. **Pick a Task**: Write down one thing you repeatedly tell yourself "only I can do," or "It's faster/better if I do it myself."
2. **Why?**: Next to it, briefly describe why you believe this is yours alone—what do you think you're bringing to the table that's "irreplaceable"?
3. **Challenge That Assumption**: Ask yourself, "Is this always true, or just true right now because I've never taught someone my process/intuition/approach?"

This exercise might feel small, but it's the first step in rewriting your mental script on delegation. You'll start seeing how many tasks could be handled by others **if** you had the right system.

Pro Tip: Share your identified task and your "why" with a trusted peer or business friend—someone outside your company who can keep you accountable. When you voice it out loud, it becomes real, and you'll be less likely to slip into denial.

Closing Thoughts

I get it: the lies we've unpacked here might sting a little. Nobody wants to admit they've built their own cage—but if you saw yourself in any of these patterns, you're in good company. I've seen countless ambitious, well-meaning founders walk right into the same trap. The difference isn't whether you fell for the lies—it's what you choose to do now that you see them.

Because here's the deal: **Most delegation advice is missing the critical piece**—it tells you to "empower your team," but never shows you how to transfer your **unique** way of thinking. That's why so many well-intentioned attempts at delegation crash and burn. It's why you end up back at your desk at midnight, redoing everyone's work.

Now that you can recognize these self-sabotaging beliefs for what they are—conscious or unconscious choices that keep you caged—it's time to understand why traditional approaches to breaking free have fallen short.

So what comes next?

In Chapter 2, we'll uncover why delegation often fails even when you're genuinely trying to make it work, and how the C.A.S.E. Method offers a fundamentally different approach.

> **Remember**: If you stay in the cage, that's your choice now. But if you dare to unlock it, get ready for the entire dynamic of your business—and your life—to change. Turn the page to see what's been holding you back from truly letting go…and why you might actually celebrate the failures that lie ahead.

CHAPTER 2 - *WHY TRADITIONAL DELEGATION FAILS*

"You do not rise to the level of your goals, you fall to the level of your systems."

—JAMES CLEAR

You've been lied to about delegation—not just once but over and over again. And if you're like most leaders I've worked with, you've already tried to "'delegate more" multiple times, only to find yourself stepping in when things inevitably went off the rails. Business books, leadership courses, management consultants—… they all tell you the same thing: 'Just delegate more.' As if the only thing standing between you and freedom is handing off more tasks.

So you try. You assign projects, create checklists, and explain how things should be done.

And yet, what happens?

Your team struggles. Mistakes pile up. You find yourself jumping in to redo their work or, worse, fixing bigger problems than if you had just done it yourself in the first place. You get frustrated, tighten your grip, and before you know it—you're back to doing everything yourself again.

And the cycle repeats.

If delegation is supposed to be the key to scaling your business and reclaiming your time, why does it so often fail?

Is Delegation Working?

The Root Problem: Delegation is Treated Like a Task, Not a System

Most delegation advice can be summed up in four bullet points:

- Write down the steps
- Create standard operating procedures (SOPs).
- Hand the task off.
- Check back in later.

Sounds reasonable, right? Except it doesn't work. Because delegation isn't about transferring *tasks*—it's about transferring *thinking.*

Right now, your team isn't struggling because they don't have checklists. They're struggling because they don't see what you see. They can't read between the lines, recognize patterns, anticipate problems, or make strategic decisions the way you do.

And that's not their fault—it's yours.

Because you've been trying to delegate the *work*, when what you really need to delegate is *how you think* about the work.

That's the critical difference. And it's where most delegation efforts fall apart.

This isn't just my observation. A 2022 study in the Harvard Business Review found that 74% of leaders who reported 'delegation failures' were focusing solely on task transfer rather than decision-making authority.

Meanwhile, those who successfully delegated thinking, not just doing, reported 41% higher team performance and 37% more personal job satisfaction.

Let's break down exactly why traditional delegation fails—and how it turns you into the very bottleneck you're trying to escape.

Why Traditional Delegation Fails (And How It's Making You the Bottleneck)

1. The Task-Execution Trap

Most traditional delegation strategies focus on breaking tasks down into steps and handing them over. But tasks are only the surface layer of work. The real magic—the part that makes you so good at what you do—is hidden beneath the surface in the form of pattern recognition, decision-making, and instinct.

When you tell someone *how* to do something but not

how to think about it, you create dependency. Every time a situation arises that isn't in the SOP, your team stops and waits for you. So, instead of doing the task, they come to you with questions—all day long.

CHAPTER 2

The Delegation Loop

Real-World Example: Mike's Midnight Ping-Pong

Mike, a startup founder, tried to delegate customer onboarding to his team. He gave them a script and checklist, but customers kept coming back to him for "special cases." His team wasn't equipped to handle the kind of situations he navigated effortlessly. Instead of freeing himself, he became the human exception handler—stuck in an endless loop of approvals and course corrections.

Mike's wake-up call came when he realized he spent more time answering his team's questions than he used to spend doing the onboarding himself. His phone would buzz at 11pm: "'Client asking about implementation timeline - what should I tell them?" Or a Slack message at 7am: "'The prospect wants to know if we can customize X feature - can we?"

Every morning, his inbox and Slack were flooded with

messages that all boiled down to the same question: "Mike, how would you handle this?"

Mike thought his people just weren't smart enough to think... he even said, 'I need you to think more.' The problem wasn't the checklist—it was that his team didn't understand why he made the decisions he did. Without that deeper insight, they were stuck second-guessing themselves—and Mike stayed stuck as the bottleneck.

While the task-execution trap keeps your team dependent on you for every exception or edge case, there's an even deeper problem: even perfect execution of steps doesn't guarantee good judgment.

2. Checklists And Sops Can't Replace Judgment

Procedures are great—for repeatable, predictable tasks. But let's be honest, most of what makes you indispensable isn't repeatable or predictable. It's a mix of intuition, experience, and quick judgment calls.

You don't follow a script when handling high-value clients, negotiating deals, or solving operational problems. You assess, adjust, and make decisions based on context. That's what your team needs to learn—not just the steps, but the thought process behind them.

Real-World Example: Emily Marketing Blindspot

Emily, a marketing agency owner, carefully documented her ad campaign process in detail. Yet, every time a new client came in, her team struggled to get the strategy right. Why? Because her real skill wasn't in following a checklist—it was in *interpreting* the brand's voice and understanding how to tweak messaging based on subtle audience insights.

One day, Emily sat in on a client pitch her team had prepared. On paper, it was perfect—hit all the right keywords, and followed the exact process she'd outlined. But something felt... off. The client wasn't engaged. That's *when it hit her: her team was executing tactics without understanding the **art** behind them. She had never broken down **why** certain messages worked and others didn't. Without that, her team was just running playbooks instead of thinking strategically.*

3. Micromanagement Masquerading As Delegation

This one is going to sting a bit. Many entrepreneurs think they're delegating when they're really just micromanaging from a distance. If you still require your team to run every decision by you, you haven't actually delegated anything—you've just turned yourself into a human bottleneck. This is the one most of us rail against. No one wants to think of themselves as a micromanager. But can I be honest with you: You are. You probably don't realize it because you have the negative connotation of micromanagement stuck in your head and not the actual definition of it. If you are 100% sure you are not a micromanager, then I dare you to take the "Am I a Micromanager?" quiz.

Scan the QR code

Or Visit:

www.TheDelegationTrap.com/resources

Real-World Example: Jason's Ownership Illusion

Jason, a software consultant, kept telling his team, "Take ownership." But every time they made a decision, he second-guessed it, changed the approach, or overruled them. The result? His employees stopped trying.

One day, his team proudly presented a new client onboarding workflow in a meeting, excited about the research they had done. Before they even finished their second slide, Jason interrupted: "Wait—why didn't you consider using an automated form?" The team had. They, in fact, researched it, but they hadn't yet gotten to that part of their presentation. Jason's impatience and his habit of constant second-guessing created a culture where no one felt confident presenting ideas. Over time, they learned to just wait for Jason to tell them what to do instead of proactively solving problems themselves.

Instinct and Intuition: The Myths That Keep You Stuck

You probably tell yourself that your instincts and intuition make you irreplaceable. That your uncanny ability to "just know" what to do can't be taught, and that's why you hesitate to fully trust your team.

But let's be real: You weren't born with this ability. You learned it. You developed it over years of experience, trial and error, and refining your judgment.

And if you *learned* it, that means others can, too.

Instinct and intuition are just highly developed pattern recognition. They're not magic—they're experience applied at speed. And experience can be transferred—if you have the right system.

The moment you stop believing you're the only one who can do something is the moment you unlock the possibility of scaling your business beyond yourself.

Action Step: Assess Your Delegation Weak Points

Take 10 minutes to list three tasks you've tried to delegate that didn't go as planned. For each one, ask yourself:

- What went wrong?
- Where did my team get stuck—execution, decision-making, or seeing the bigger picture?
- How could I have better transferred my thinking instead of just the task?

The C.A.S.E. Method: A New Way to Delegate

The C.A.S.E. Method is a new way to delegate. Traditional delegation methods focus on output: getting someone else to execute a task. But the C.A.S.E. Method is fundamentally different. It focuses on input—teaching your team how to process information, recognize patterns, and make decisions like you would. Instead of saying, 'Do it like this,' The C.A.S.E. Method asks your team to walk through four key questions that transform them from order-takers into independent thinkers:

1. **C – Challenge:** *What obstacles did you face in completing this task?*
2. **A – Articulate:** *What steps did you take, and why?*
3. **S – Study:** *What guided your choices, and what did you learn?*
4. **E – Easier Than Expected:** *What parts came naturally, and why?*

Now that you understand why traditional delegation

fails—and why it's been trapped in the founder's cage despite your best efforts—it's time to choose your first task for the C.A.S.E. Method. But this won't be the kind of task most delegation experts recommend. In fact, in Chapter 3, I'm going to ask you to do something that might feel counterintuitive, even risky. Turn the page to discover which task will give you the most leverage in breaking free from your self-made cage.

Turn the page, and let's dive into the system that will finally set you free.

CHAPTER 3 - *CHOOSING YOUR FIRST C.A.S.E. TASK*

"Start with something small. Begin with the easy stuff. Delegate the basic tasks first."

If you've read any business advice about delegation, you've probably heard these suggestions. And they're completely wrong for what we're trying to accomplish.

Why Small Tasks Don't Create Big Changes

Think about it: If you delegate answering emails or scheduling meetings, what really changes in your organization? You might free up an hour or two in your day, but you're still the bottleneck for everything important. You're still the only one who can close the big deals, handle the high-stakes client relationships, make the strategic decisions, and solve the complex problems. In other words, you've tidied your cage but remain firmly locked inside it. The reason most delegation efforts fail is that they start with the least consequential tasks—ones that, even when perfectly executed, don't meaningfully reduce your workload or develop your team's capabilities. You're exchanging minor administrative burdens for the new burden of checking and correcting someone else's work on those small tasks.

CHOOSING YOUR FIRST
C.A.S.E. TASK

In other words, you're still trapped.

The reason most entrepreneurs get delegation wrong is that they start by handing off *tasks* instead of *thinking*. They outsource execution while keeping all decision-making locked in their own heads.

So, we're going to do something different.

The Counterintuitive Approach

I want you to do something that might feel scary: Choose a task that makes you nervous to let go.

Seriously—pick something that feels too important. Something that makes your stomach tighten at the thought of someone else doing it. A task that feels like it's tied directly to your identity, your standards, or your value.

Why? Because that's where your unique genius hides.

When you feel that resistance, that fear of letting go, you've found something valuable. That tension means you're at the edge of real transformation—not just time management.

Workbook Exercise: Building on Your Previous Work

Open your **C.A.S.E. Method Workbook** at (www.TheDelegationTrap.com/workbook).

Go to the section where you listed the tasks you've attempted to delegate before (from Chapter 2). If you haven't completed that exercise yet, go back and do it now before continuing.

Now, take that list and apply the following decision framework to choose the right task for your first C.A.S.E. Method implementation.

The Five Filters for Choosing Your First Task

Not every "only I can do this" task is right for your

first C.A.S.E. Method implementation. Run your circled items through these five filters in your workbook:

1. High-Impact, High-Frequency

Ask yourself:

- Does this task significantly affect your business outcomes or client relationships?
- Does it occur regularly enough (at least monthly) to justify the investment in training?
- Would successfully delegating it create a noticeable difference in your workload or business operations?

High-impact tasks touch your core business functions—they affect revenue, client satisfaction, or team performance. When delegated successfully, these create immediate breathing room in your schedule while developing critical capabilities in your team. The frequency component matters because you want sufficient repetition for your team member to practice and refine their approach.

One-off projects might be important, but they don't create sustainable shifts in your workload patterns. Look for tasks where successful delegation would make you think, "Wow, I can't believe I don't have to handle that anymore."

2. Requires Critical Thinking

Ask yourself:

- Does this task involve significant decision-making rather than just following instructions?
- Does it require someone to apply judgment, context, or expertise?
- Would someone need to understand the underlying principles rather than just following the steps?

The most valuable delegation involves transferring thinking, not just doing. Tasks that require critical thinking are the ones where you typically find yourself saying, "It depends," when someone asks how to handle a situation. These tasks can't be reduced to a flowchart or checklist because they involve weighing multiple factors, considering context, and making judgment calls.

The richness of these tasks makes them perfect for the C.A.S.E. Method because they require your team members to understand your thought process, not just mimic your actions. When you delegate these tasks, you're transferring not just responsibility but real intellectual capital.

3. Makes You Nervous To Let Go

Ask yourself:

- Do you feel a twinge of anxiety when you think about someone else handling this?
- Have you avoided delegating this because "it's just easier to do it myself"?

- Do you habitually check, redo, or significantly edit others' work in this area?

This discomfort is actually a powerful indicator that you've found the right task. The nervous feeling typically stems from one of two sources: either the task truly matters (confirming Filter #1), or you've become emotionally attached to doing it "your way." Both signals point to an opportunity for meaningful delegation.

The tasks that make you nervous are often the ones where you've developed sophisticated but unconscious expertise—exactly the kind of thinking the C.A.S.E. Method helps you transfer. Pay special attention to areas where you frequently find yourself saying, "Let me take a look at that before it goes out," as these represent your tightest control points.

4. Has Clear Outcomes

Ask yourself:

- Can you articulate what "success" looks like for this task?
- Are there objective ways to measure whether it's been done well?
- Would another person be able to self-evaluate their performance?

Tasks with clear outcomes provide a crucial learning framework for your team. When success criteria are vague or exist only in your head, delegation becomes a frustrating guessing game where your team member can never quite "get it right."

Clear outcomes don't mean simple ones—complex tasks can still have well-defined success parameters. Look for tasks where you can say, "Here's how we'll know this worked," whether that's through client feedback, measurable metrics, or specific deliverable characteristics. This clarity creates confidence for your team member and reduces the need for constant check-ins, accelerating their path to true ownership.

5. Room For Improvement

Ask yourself:

- Is there potential for someone to bring fresh insights or approaches to this task?
- Are there aspects of how you currently handle it that could be more efficient or effective?
- Would a different perspective potentially yield better results than your current approach?

The most powerful delegation happens when you're open to your process being improved. Tasks you've been handling with a "this is how we've always done it" thinking are prime candidates. When you delegate a task that has room for improvement, you create space for innovation while acknowledging that your way might not be the only—or even the best—approach.

This openness transforms delegation from a burden (teaching someone to replicate your methods) into an opportunity (discovering better methods together). It also signals to your team member that you value their thinking, not just their ability to follow directions, which dramatically increases their investment in the outcome.

Workbook Exercise: Choosing Your First Task

By now, you should have several potential tasks identified. Choose one that:

1. Meets at least 4 of the 5 filters
2. Would free up significant time if delegated
3. Could be transformative for your business
4. **Is NOT client-facing**—we want to avoid adding unnecessary anxiety in this first step.

Write down your selected task in the designated section of your C.A.S.E. Method Workbook. If you haven't already downloaded it, you can get your copy at:

www.TheDelegationTrap.com/Workbook

Common Task Categories to Consider

When choosing your first task, focus on areas such as:

- Strategic decision-making
- Internal operations
- Process improvement
- Team management and training
- System development
- Quality control
- Technical expertise

What Not to Choose

Avoid tasks that:

- Are purely administrative
- Follow rigid, step-by-step procedures
- Don't require judgment or problem-solving
- Are already well-documented
- Offer little or no room for improvement
- Occur rarely or irregularly
- **Are client-facing at this stage**—and here's

why we're not starting there. You're already taking a huge step by recognizing that you might have been micromanaging more than you thought. That realization alone can shake how you see yourself, your team, and your ability to lead. I'm not asking you to go cold turkey on micromanaging—delegation is a muscle, and we need to build it in a way that sets you up for success, not panic.

Client-facing tasks add an extra layer of anxiety because they involve external perception and potential financial stakes. Right now, we're focusing on internal tasks where the stakes feel more manageable, so you can build trust in the process before moving to higher-pressure responsibilities. Think of this as a controlled environment for testing, refining, and building confidence in the C.A.S.E. Method before applying it externally.

Workbook Exercise: Finalizing

Your Task Choice

Revisit your workbook and confirm your chosen task. Answer the following questions:

1. What makes this task challenging to delegate?
2. What specific fears or concerns do you have about handing it off?
3. What would happen if you successfully delegated this task?

The Path Forward

Take a moment to sit with the task you've chosen. Notice any resistance rising within you. That discomfort? It's not a red flag—it's confirmation that you've picked the right challenge.

Before moving on, turn to your workbook and complete this section. Take a moment to journal the feelings you're experiencing right now. What emotions are coming up as you prepare to hand off this task? Are you feeling excitement, anxiety, relief, or hesitation?

Write down any thoughts about how this shift in delegation is challenging or changing how you see yourself as a leader. This is an important part of your growth—acknowledging and processing these emotions will help you step into your next phase of leadership with clarity and confidence.

Remember: We're not looking for small changes. We're creating transformation.

In the coming chapters, we'll walk through exactly how to hand off this task using the C.A.S.E. Method. You'll learn:

- How to document your process without getting overwhelmed
- The right way to set expectations
- How to prepare for your first C.A.S.E. Method meeting

First though, in the next chapter, I want to share a

secret weapon that will guarantee your success.

Turn the page when you're ready to step into a new way of leading.

CHAPTER 4 - *WHY YOU NEED AN ACCOUNTABILITY PARTNER (OUTSIDE YOUR BUSINESS)*

"You Can't Solve This Alone"

If you've read this far, it means you're serious about breaking free from the founder's trap. You understand now that delegation isn't just about handing off tasks—it's about transferring your thinking. You're beginning to see that the problem isn't your team; it's the way you've been approaching leadership.

But here's the uncomfortable truth: Your brain is wired to sabotage this effort. When you try to change deep-seated habits—especially those tied to your identity as the person who 'handles everything'—your mind will generate perfectly reasonable excuses to revert to old patterns. "This client is too important to risk." 'We're in a critical growth phase.' 'I'll delegate more next quarter when things calm down.' Without someone to call you out on these rationalizations, you'll find yourself back in the same overwhelmed state within weeks, wondering why "delegation doesn't work for your business".

That's why you need an accountability partner. And no, not someone within your team. You need a fellow entrepreneur—someone who understands what it's like to carry the weight of a business, who knows how hard it is to let go, and who will call you out when you start making excuses.

Why You Need Someone Outside Your Organization

Your employees, managers, and even business partners offer the kind of unfiltered accountability required for real change. Here's why: They operate within the power dynamics you've established. Even with the best intentions, they're unlikely to push back when you say, 'I need to handle this client personally' or 'We'll implement delegation after this quarter's rush.'

This is where the Escape the Cage Triad comes in—a structured relationship with two fellow business owners who face similar challenges but have no stake in your daily operations. They can spot your self-sabotage patterns from a mile away because they've used those same excuses themselves.

Instead, your accountability partners should be other business owners or leaders—someone who has no stake in your daily operations but understands your struggles firsthand. This person will:

- **Challenge your thinking** when you slip back

into micromanagement.
- **Call you out** when you make excuses like, "I don't have time to train them."
- **Remind you of your commitment** when you're tempted to take back control.
- **Celebrate your progress** when you start seeing results.

The Power of the Accountability Triad

While having one accountability partner is powerful, research shows that three is even better than two. According to a comprehensive 2023 study published by the American Society of Training and Development (ASTD), accountability increases commitment to action by 65% when you commit to someone else. However, when structured in a group of three, this commitment jumps to over 95%.

Why? The psychology is fascinating. With just one partner, it's easy to rationalize skipping a check-in now and then. But when **two other people are expecting you to show up**, the social pressure kicks in. You don't want to be the one who didn't follow through when the others did.

I call these **Escape the Cage Triads**—a system where

three entrepreneurs hold each other accountable in a structured way as they implement the C.A.S.E Method. It's a system designed to ensure greater consistency and a diversity of perspectives.

Why Three Is Better Than Two

1. **Diverse Perspectives** – Two people may reinforce each other's blind spots. With three, you gain an extra layer of insight and a broader range of experiences.
2. **Less Pressure on One Person** – If one accountability partner is unavailable, the other two can still meet and ensure consistency.
3. **Increased Commitment** – The group dynamic naturally makes people more likely to follow through. When two people expect you to show up and be accountable, you're less likely to drop the ball.

How the Accountability Triad Works

1. **Meet Weekly or Bi-Weekly** – Keep it short (20-30 minutes). The goal is consistency, not marathon sessions.
2. **Prepare for C.A.S.E. Method Meetings** – One of the biggest failures in delegation isn't the system—it's the leader's mindset before going into the meeting. Use triad check-ins to process challenges in advance so you show up clear-headed and ready.
3. **Ask the Right Questions** – Each member should challenge the others with the **Accountability Questions** (see the next section). This ensures no one is dodging the hard truths or falls back into old habits.

The First Step: Share This Book

Here are your first action steps to build your accountability triad:

1. **Identify two people who could be your accountability partners.**
2. **Share this book with them. (see sample messaging below)**
3. Open your workbook and write down their names. This commitment will make your accountability real from day one.

Here's a sample message you can send to your prospective accountability partners:

Sample Text Message:
"Hey, I'm reading *The C.A.S.E. Method* and realizing I've built a cage around myself—I've trapped myself in my business because I've been delegating all wrong. I'm committed to getting free of my "cage" but I need help. Would you be willing to be my accountability partner? Here's a link to check it out:

www.TheDelegationTrap.com/Triad

The site has a free chapter, a podcast episode, and a short video that explains the method. Let's make this happen together!"

On the website, your potential accountability partners will find:

- **Chapter 1 for free** so they can quickly understand what this book is about.
- **A podcast episode** where I break down The C.A.S.E. Method in a conversation with another entrepreneur.
- **A short video** of me explaining the core concept of The C.A.S.E. Method.

Share the link, explain why you're making this change, and invite them to join you. You'll be surprised by how many business owners are struggling with the exact same problem—and are ready to take action.

The Questions You Should Ask Each Other

To make your accountability meetings powerful catalysts for change rather than casual check-ins, focus on these penetrating questions:

1. Evidence of Progress or Retreat

- 'What specific task did you delegate this week that you would normally have handled yourself?'
- 'Where did you feel the urge to step in and "fix" something, and what did you do instead?'

2 Mindset Excavation

- 'What story did you tell yourself when you felt resistance to delegation?'
- 'What triggered your biggest delegation discomfort this week?'

3. Strategy Refinement

- 'What will you delegate next week that stretches your comfort zone?'

- 'How will you prepare differently for your next C.A.S.E. conversation based on what you learned?'

4. Commitment Crystallization

- 'What is one thing we should call you out on if we hear it in our next conversation?'
- 'What specific result will you report back to us by our next meeting?'

These questions transform accountability from vague encouragement into strategic intervention, targeting exactly where your old habits try to reassert control."

The Big Commitment

I know you might be thinking, "I don't have time for this." But let me ask you this:

- Do you have time to keep working 60+ hours

a week because you refuse to let go?
- Do you have time to stay trapped in a business that can't function without you?
- Do you have time to be the bottleneck that holds back your company's growth?

Because that's what happens when you don't commit to change.

If you're serious about transforming how you lead, then you'll take five minutes right now to send a message to **two fellow entrepreneurs** and invite them to do this with you.

This is where real change starts. Because reading this book won't change your business—**but what you do next will.**

Moving Forward

Now that you've identified your first meaningful task to delegate and chosen your accountability partners, you're ready for the moment of truth: the actual handoff.

In Chapter 5, you'll learn exactly how to transfer responsibility in a way that empowers your team members for success without creating dependence on you. The specific words, timing, and structure of this handoff will determine whether you're truly delegating thinking or just assigning tasks. Turn the page when you're ready to take this crucial step.

CHAPTER 5 - *HANDING OFF YOUR FIRST C.A.S.E METHOD TASK WITHOUT LOSING CONTROL*

The Critical Moment: Choosing the Right Person

So, you've chosen the task you're going to delegate. You've shared that decision with your accountability partners. Now comes the moment of truth—the actual handoff.

This is where most delegation efforts are all apart. Too often, the task is assigned in a hurried conversation, with vague expectations and incomplete instructions. The result? Confusion, disappointment, and—eventually—you taking the task back with a sigh and the familiar thought, 'I should have just done it myself.' But that's not your path. You're about to take a fundamentally different approach—one that sets both you and your team members up for success from the start. And it begins with something most delegation advice completely overlooks: choosing the right person for this specific task.

Let's be clear: **not everyone on your team is ready for every task**. Just because someone has time doesn't mean they're the right fit. And just because someone has the technical ability doesn't mean they have the judgment to execute well. Your job is to pick wisely.

Here's how:

The 4-Point Selection Framework

Before handing off any task, run your potential candidates through this four-point filter. This ensures you're not just delegating to the most available person—but to the *right* one.

1. Capacity To Learn

Look for evidence in past interactions: Has this person shown the ability to take and incorporate your feedback? When you've offered suggestions, do they typically implement them or resist?

A great candidate for the C.A.S.E. Method sees feedback as a gift, not a personal attack. They're open, coachable, and willing to grow.

Pay attention to how they respond to new information. Do they ask clarifying questions or connect new concepts to what they already know? Are they engaged enough to paraphrase your instructions or ask thoughtful follow-up questions? The ideal candidate doesn't just nod along—they actively process information by paraphrasing it back to you or asking about implications.

Watch for phrases like "That's a good point" or "I hadn't thought of it that way" versus defensive responses like "But I did it this way because..." or "That wouldn't have worked because..."

Also, consider how they've handled previous learning curves. Did they persist through difficulty, or did they quickly become frustrated and give up? The C.A.S.E. Method requires patience and resilience through multiple iterations—someone who expects instant mastery will struggle with this process.

2. Attention To Detail

This isn't about perfectionism but rather awareness of what matters in a particular context. Observe how this person handles existing responsibilities:

Do they catch important nuances without being prompted? Are they aware of potential risks or inconsistencies before they escalate?

Review recent work they've completed. Do they tend to overlook the same types of details—like technical specs, client preferences, or timelines? If so, be cautious when assigning tasks that require sharp awareness in those areas.

Test their observational skills by asking them to review something with multiple layers of complexity. Those who only catch surface-level issues might not be ready for tasks requiring depth of analysis.

The right candidate doesn't need to catch everything, but they should demonstrate an ability to identify which details are mission-critical versus which are preferences. This level of discernment is crucial for independent decision-making.

3. Initiative To Solve Problems

This one is big. Initiative isn't just about working hard—it's about how someone approaches obstacles.

Consider: When this person encounters a roadblock, do they immediately come to you for solutions—or do they first attempt to resolve it on their own?

Look for evidence of resourcefulness. Have they ever surprised you with a clever workaround or fixed an issue before you even knew it existed? These are strong indicators of problem-solving initiative.

Also, evaluate their question patterns. Do they ask open-ended questions that show they're trying to understand underlying principles—do they ask closed questions that simply seek your approval or direction? The former indicates someone who wants to understand why, not just what to do.

The ideal candidate shows curiosity about how things work and why certain approaches are taken. They might say things like "I was wondering if we could try..." or "I found a different approach that might work because..." rather than "Just tell me what you want me to do." You need thinkers, not just doers.

4. Willingness To Receive Feedback

This might be the most important factor of all. Delegation through the C.A.S.E. Method involves multiple feedback cycles—if someone shuts down or becomes defensive or when receiving constructive criticism, the entire process will stall.

Also, notice how this person has responded to feedback in the past. Do they thank you for pointing out areas of improvement? Do they ask follow-up questions to understand feedback more deeply? Or do they become quiet, argumentative, or visibly upset?

Consider how they handle public versus private feedback. Some people process criticism better in private conversations where they don't feel exposed. This doesn't disqualify them—it just means you should structure your C.A.S.E. meetings accordingly.

What matters most is their mindset. Someone who says "I'd like to get better at that" rather than "That's just not my strength" is showing the growth mindset essential for the C.A.S.E. Method to work effectively.

Lastly, pay attention to whether they implement feedback over time. The best candidates might not get it right immediately after feedback, but they make consistent progress toward incorporating your guidance, showing they value the input even when it's challenging.

Warning: Don't default to "who has the most free time." That's a common recipe for failure. Free time doesn't mean they have the **right** skills.

What If No One on Your

Team Feels Right?

If you're struggling to find someone who fits, you've got a bigger issue: **you haven't properly developed your team.** This book isn't just about fixing delegation—it's about building a culture where people can step up. If no one seems ready, choose the best available option and commit to developing them. Train them like you would train your future second-in-command. It's an investment in your future capacity.

The Handoff Meeting: It's Not a Quick Chat—It's a Formal Process

Most entrepreneurs screw up delegation at the handoff. They casually drop a task on someone's desk in between meetings or fire off a Slack message like, "Hey, can you handle this?"

That's lazy delegation. And lazy delegation creates disasters.

Instead, you need a **formal, scheduled handoff meeting.** Treat it like a critical project kickoff, not a sidebar conversation.

The 5 Steps to a Successful Handoff Meeting

A successful handoff doesn't start in the meeting—it starts with **you doing the pre-work**. Before you even sit down with your team member, you need to:

- **Document the process–** Write down as many steps as possible that you take to complete the task. Be detailed, but don't worry about making it perfect. Just get your process on paper.
- **Accept imperfection–** Acknowledge that failure is part of the process. Your employees *will* struggle, and that's expected. The goal is not perfection—it's learning and improving.
- **Set growth-based expectations–** Set the right expectations by making it clear that the process will evolve and their job is to help refine it.

Once you've done the prep work, here's how to run the meeting so your team actually takes ownership:

1. **Set Clear Expectations**
    - The focus is on following the process, not achieving perfection.
    - Expect big, gross errors at first—this is

part of the learning curve.
- They are not being judged on the outcome but on their effort in executing and refining the process.
- Here's how this conversation might sound: **You**: 'I want to be clear about something upfront, Michael. I'm not expecting perfection on the first attempt—or even the third. What I'm looking for is your engagement with the process and your willingness to learn from whatever happens.'

Michael: 'So if I make mistakes...?'

You: 'When you encounter obstacles—because you will—I want you to document them. Those aren't failures; they're data points that help us refine the process. The real failure would be hiding problems or giving up when things get tough.'

Michael: 'That's a relief. I was worried

about messing up such an important task.'

You: 'The task is important, but your development is even more important. I'd rather you try, struggle, and learn than play it safe and depend on me for every decision.

2. **Explain the Why (Not Just the How)**

    o   Why does this task matter?

    o   How does it connect to the bigger business goals?

    o   What's at stake if the process is ignored or not followed correctly?

3. **Outline Resources & Boundaries**

    o   What tools, templates or documents do they need?

    o   Where can they find answers if they get stuck?

    o   What decisions can they make

on their own vs. which require your approval?

Clarity reduces dependency and empowers action.

4. **Commit to a C.A.S.E Method Meeting**

    o   Set a date for the first C.A.S.E review session before they start.
    o   Reinforce that mistakes are expected (but learning is required).
    o   Let them know they will not be judged on the outcome, but rather on their effort to follow and improve the process.

5. **Shut Up and Let Them Own It**

    o   Stop hovering.
    o   Don't check in every five minutes.
    o   Let them work through the initial roadblocks without rescuing them.

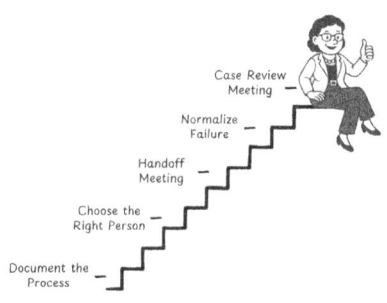

The Silent Killer: Taking the Task Back

This is where founders fail. The moment things don't go perfectly, they grab the task back.

Here's the rule: **Once you delegate, you can't touch the task again.** You can review and coach in your C.A.S.E Method meeting, but you **cannot** step in and "fix" things yourself. Doing so will destroy the whole process.

If they struggle, great—that's the point. Let them figure it out. That's how they learn. If they completely screw it up? Use the C.A.S.E Method meeting to diagnose and improve. But **do not take it back.**

The Next Step: Your First C.A.S.E Method Meeting

Once they've completed the task, you don't immediately review their work—you hold a C.A.S.E. Method meeting. This is where the magic happens. Instead of simply giving feedback on what they did right or wrong, you'll guide them through a structured conversation that reveals how they think.

Schedule this meeting before they even begin the task. Put it on both your calendars as a non-negotiable appointment, ideally within 48 hours of task completion. This sends a powerful message: the conversation about the work is as important as the work itself.

In the next chapter, I'll show you exactly how to run that meeting like a pro, so your team starts thinking at your level—without you being the bottleneck. You'll learn the specific questions that transform task-takers into problem-solvers and how to respond when they inevitably approach the task differently than you would have.

In the next chapter, I'll show you how to lead this meeting like a pro—so your team starts thinking at your level, without you becoming the bottleneck. You'll get the exact questions that turn task-doers into strategic thinkers, and how to handle them when they approach the task differently than you would.

Action Steps:

1. **Pick the Right Person** – Run candidates through the 4-Point Selection Framework.
2. **Schedule the Handoff Meeting** – Do not delegate over Slack or in a casual chat.

3. **Commit to Hands-Off Delegation** – No taking the task back once it's handed off.
4. **Book Your First C.A.S.E Meeting** – Put it on the calendar **before** they start the task.
5. **Do the Pre-Work** – Write down your steps and set expectations for failure as a learning tool.
6. **Document & Share** – Record your delegation plan and share it with your accountability triad.

Ready to see how C.A.S.E transforms this into a long-term system that scales your leadership? Flip the page.

CHAPTER 6 - *RUNNING YOUR FIRST C.A.S.E. METHOD MEETING—TURNING TASK-TAKERS INTO THINKERS*

"People support what they create"

- BRENDON BURCHARD

You've done the hard part. You picked your first C.A.S.E. Method task—something that used to make your stomach do flips when you thought about letting someone else handle it. You bounced it off your "Escape the Cage" Triad, got their feedback and officially handed off the task in a well-structured meeting with clear expectations.

Now comes the defining moment—the one that separates true delegation from mere task assignment: the C.A.S.E. Method meeting. This isn't just another check-in or status update. This conversation is where the magic happens—where you transform someone from following directions to understanding principles, from executing tasks to internalizing your thinking process.

When done right, this meeting won't just reduce your workload on *this* task—it will pave the way for dozens of decisions your team members will soon be able to make *without* needing you at all.

Your Mindset: The Hidden Key to C.A.S.E. Success

Before you walk into your first C.A.S.E. meeting, a critical shift needs to happen in your own thinking.

You must temporarily suspend your identity as the answer-provider and solution-creator. In this meeting, your role flips. You are no longer the boss correcting errors—you are:

- You are an investigator, not a judge.
- You are a mirror, not a director.
- You are a curious observer, not an anxious owner.

This mental shift is profoundly uncomfortable for most founders and executives. Your success to date has likely come from having great answers, making quick decisions, and setting high standards.

But in the C.A.S.E. meeting, those strengths can work against you if they lead you to dominate the conversation or rush to correction. Remind yourself before the meeting: 'My goal is not to fix their work. My goal is to understand their thinking process—so I can help them develop judgment, not just follow my instructions.' This mindset shift takes conscious practice. Many leaders find it helpful to literally write these reminders on a notecard that they glance at during the meeting when they feel the urge to take control of the conversation.

WHAT MAKES A C.A.S.E. METHOD MEETING DIFFERENT?

Let's first clarify what this meeting is **not**:

- It's **not** a quick "So, how'd it go?" hallway chat.
- It's **not** a chance for you to unload a wave of edits and corrections while your team member silently jots down notes.
- It's **not** an unplanned "drive-by debrief" tacked on to another meeting.

A C.A.S.E. Method meeting is **a scheduled, structured conversation** designed to turn an "okay" handoff into a significant leap in your team member's ability to think. The entire framework revolves around four questions. Each letter in C.A.S.E Method represents a core question you'll walk through with your team member:

1. **C – Challenge**
2. **A – Articulate**
3. **S** – Study
4. **E – Easier Than Expected**

Where the usual founder-led meeting might be you micromanaging or redoing tasks, this approach is all about **excavating your team's thought process**. If you do it right, you'll transform them from mere doers into confident decision-makers.

Next, we'll break down how to lead the conversation around each of these four questions so you get more than just answers—you get insight.

Are you ready to run your first real C.A.S.E. Method meeting?

THE ANATOMY OF A C.A.S.E.

METHOD MEETING

Let's break down the four key questions that form the structure of a C.A.S.E. Method meeting You'll walk through them in order, letting your team member do **most** of the talking.

1. C – Challenge (10 Minutes)

Prompt: "What challenges did you face in completing this task?"

This first question is powerful. You start by focusing on **obstacles** or **problems** because it immediately tells your team: *"I want to hear what you experienced."* I'm sure you have asked this question before but your intent was not to truly understand what they experienced from their perspective. Your intent was to figure out what needed to be fixed.

Let me be blunt: your only job when you ask this question is to shut up and take notes. Do not interject. No advice. No suggestions. No praise. No corrections. Just listen. You're allowed to ask the follow up questions listed below. Truly listen to what they say. You are attempting to gain an understanding of how they think and why they made certain choices. Do not ruin the meeting by playing savior or smartest person in the room and interjecting your thoughts, ideas, or corrections.

- Your Role:
    - Keep quiet. Really. Listen actively and maintain a neutral expression (yes, practice your poker face).
    - Don't fix anything yet—resist the urge.
    - Write notes on their challenges. (I've included a C.A.S.E Method meeting template in your workbook)

- **Helpful Follow-Up Questions**:
    - "Which parts of the process felt unclear?"
    - "Where did you feel stuck or second-guessing your decisions?"

2. A – Articulate (15 Minutes)

Prompt: "Walk me through exactly how you did this, step by step."

Again, your role here is to listen and take notes—nothing more. Don't interrupt for clarification. Don't react. Don't evaluate. Just absorb.

The aim of this question is to get them to give you a **chronological** rundown of what they did:

- Did they open a certain spreadsheet?
- Did they run certain scripts or ask a colleague for data?
- Did they reorder tasks in a particular way?
- Did they skip or invent steps you never told

them about?

You're not going through the final product. You're dissecting the **process**.

As they share their steps, you will see 4 things, the last 2 are the most important:

1. Steps they did correctly
2. Steps they did incorrectly
3. Assumptions they made and the choices that caused
4. Assumptions YOU make at certain steps that cause you to make different choices

This begins to shape the picture of how they think versus how you think, and once we understand that, we can build a bridge to help them understand your thinking.

3. S – Study (15 Minutes)

Prompt: "Why did you make those choices, and what guided your thinking?"

Now that you've heard *what* they did, it's time to

understand *why*. This is where the real transformation begins. The Articulate step gave you a clear picture of the steps your team member took. Choose two steps they did correctly and two steps they did incorrectly. The maximum number of steps you should analyze in a C.A.S.E Method meeting is four. Are there more than four steps you need to "help" them with...absolutely...AND this is not the time. As we will discuss later C.A.S.E Method is an interactive process.

It's more important to go through the steps the team members did correctly than the ones they did incorrectly. If you ran the C.A.S.E Method kickoff meeting correctly, then you prepared the employee for failure; now it's time to show them it was not ALL failure. Any boss can sit for an hour and talk about the things you did wrong; few try to understand your thinking about the things you did correctly.

Ok, so how do we do this deep dive study into the four steps:

    1. Choose the 4 steps you want to deep dive into

2. Ask these questions
    1. Based on the previous step, why did you make this choice?
    2. What other factors affected your making this choice?
    3. Was the outcome of this step what you expected?
    4. How did the outcome of this step affect the overall process?

When you had the team member articulate their steps, you started to get a glimpse of where their misunderstandings lie and a deeper understanding of the micro decisions you make as you complete these steps.

What you are looking for is:

- **Knowledge gaps**: They made an assumption about how the data was updated or which tool was "standard."
- **Misinterpretations**: They might have read your instructions in a way you never intended.
- **Shining insights**: Maybe they combined steps or tried a new method that could actually improve the process.

Resist the urge to judge. Approach it like a detective: "Oh, that's interesting. So you re-labeled the columns because you thought it matched up with last quarter's layout. Why did you think they needed to match last quarter?" Notice that was a question, not a statement. When a team member is learning and you are helping them think differently, it's better to ask questions and not make statements.

By now, you should be able to clearly see the GAP between their thinking and yours. Use questions to help them think through and understand from a different perspective. In the next chapter, we will dive deep into the types of questions to ask.

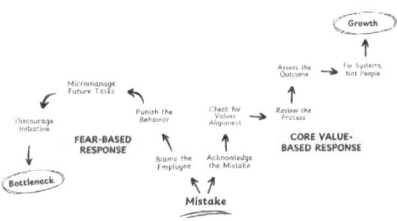

Pitfalls to Avoid

Leading Questions

As you explore your team member's thinking process, how you phrase your questions is critical. Avoid leading questions that telegraph the 'right' answer: 'Don't you think you should have checked with accounting first?' Instead, use open-ended, curiosity-driven questions:

• 'What factors did you consider when deciding to move

forward without checking with accounting?'

• 'How did you prioritize speed versus stakeholder alignment in this situation?'

• 'What precedents or past experiences informed that decision?' Notice these questions don't indicate whether their approach was right or wrong—they simply explore the thinking process. This creates psychological safety that encourages honest reflection rather than defensive justification.

Shaming

If you find a big hole in their reasoning, don't label it "stupid." Instead, help them see the correct principle. Chances are when you truly understand their perspective, you will "agree" with the choices they made, even if they were wrong. Try saying:

"I see why you concluded that. Here's the typical logic we follow so we don't confuse data sets. Next time, let's factor that in."

4. E – Easier Than Expected (10 Minutes)

Prompt: "Which parts came more naturally, or ended up simpler than you anticipated—and why do you think that was?"

At first glance, this question seems trivial. **It's not.** Here's why:

1. **Highlights Hidden Strengths**: They might have found chart formatting or data analysis easy—something you personally find tedious. That's a strength worth leveraging.
2. **Reveals Potential Upgrades**: If they breezed through a step that you used to dread, maybe they can refine that step further or teach it to others.
3. **Builds Confidence**: Ending on a positive note of "Hey, I *did* do something well" helps them leave the meeting energized, not deflated.

Pitfall To Avoid

Forgetting to Celebrate Wins: Even if their "easy" part is something you consider minor, don't just brush it aside. A small success can be a gateway to bigger innovations.

When Things Go Sideways: Course-Correcting the Conversation

Even with the best intentions, it's easy to slip into old patterns during these meetings. Here are some common derailments and how to get back on track:

- **Instead of:** 'You should have checked with accounting before finalizing these numbers.'

    Try: 'I'm curious about the verification process you used for these numbers. Can you walk me through your approach?'

- **Instead of:** 'This section doesn't align with our brand voice at all.'

    Try: 'When you were writing this section, what were you using as a reference for our brand voice?'

- **Instead of:** 'Why didn't you use the template I showed you last month?'

    Try: 'What resources or references did you consider when formatting this document?'

- **Instead of:** 'Let me just fix this part for you.'

    Try: 'This part seems to be creating a challenge. What support would help you approach it differently next time?'

Notice that effective responses maintain curiosity, avoid blame, and keep the focus on learning rather than correction. They invite explanations rather than shutting down the conversation.

Document the Takeaways:
Creating a Learning Legacy

The insights from your C.A.S.E. meeting are far too valuable to trust to memory. Create a living document that captures:

- **Process Insights:** What specific steps need clarification or modification based on this conversation?
- **Decision Principles:** What key decision-making frameworks emerged that could guide future choices?
- **Knowledge Gaps:** What additional information, training, or resources would strengthen their capabilities?
- **Success Patterns:** What approaches worked well and should be reinforced?

Updating The Original Process Document

One of the most important steps after a C.A.S.E. Method meeting is to revisit the original process documentation you shared during the handoff. That document likely had blind spots—maybe even intentionally so, as it represented your internalized workflow, not a comprehensive manual.

Now is the time to transform that imperfect guide into something truly valuable:

1. **Collaborative Refinement:** Have your team members contribute to updating the document based on what they learned through experience. Their fresh perspective will identify gaps you've become blind to over time.
2. **Adding Decision Points:** Update the documentation to include not just what to do, but how to make decisions at critical junctures. For instance, "At this stage, consider X, Y, and Z factors to determine priority."
3. **Incorporating Real Examples:** Add specific examples from their work that illustrate both successful approaches and common pitfalls.
4. **From Checklist to Playbook:** Evolve the document from a simple procedural checklist to a strategic playbook that future team members can use to develop judgment, not just complete tasks.

This documentation serves several critical purposes:

1. It transforms a single conversation into a reference resource for future tasks.
2. It creates institutional knowledge that can be shared with others who might take on similar responsibilities.
3. It provides a baseline for measuring growth over subsequent C.A.S.E. conversations.
4. It demonstrates to your team member that this isn't just talk—you're committed to their development through a systematic process.
5. It gradually builds a library of well-documented processes that reduce your business's dependence on any single person's knowledge—including yours.

The most effective format is a shared document that both you and your team members can access and update. After each C.A.S.E. meeting, allow them to add their own insights first, then supplement them with your observations. This co-creation reinforces their ownership of the learning process and ensures the document reflects both experiential knowledge and strategic principles.

Scan the QR code

OR

Visit *www.TheDelegationTrap.com/Resources* for an SOP template.

COMMON PITFALLS & HOW TO AVOID THEM

Pitfall: Conflating This With A Performance Review

If your team members think you're grading them, they'll hide mistakes. Emphasize that mistakes = data for improvement. Actual performance reviews should happen separately or at a different time so they can be fully honest here.

Pitfall: Hovering During The Task

If you ride a shotgun while they try to do the work, you won't learn anything about how they truly think. Next time, step away. Let them wrestle with the work. You'll get far better insight into their process—and they'll grow faster from the challenge.

Pitfall: Omitting The "Easier Than Expected" Question

It's tempting to skip the positivity—especially if you see glaring errors. But skipping it robs you both of discovering new strengths. Don't overlook it.

Pitfall: Declaring Victory Too Soon

One good meeting doesn't fix everything. Real delegation mastery evolves over multiple cycles. Keep scheduling C.A.S.E. sessions until the process is so strong you barely need them.

REAL-LIFE INTERNAL EXAMPLES (NO CLIENTS INVOLVED)

The Weekly Data Report That Freed Up The Founder

Scenario

- **Task**: The founder used to create a weekly internal data report to share with the team.

- **Handoff**: He chose a data-savvy junior but worried about "quality control."

- **Triad Approval**: His accountability partners challenged him: "Great. That's a recurring, high-impact task that you do every Monday. Perfect to delegate."

First C.a.s.e. Method Meeting

- **Challenges (C)**: The junior felt uncertain about which metrics truly mattered and got confused by old spreadsheet tabs the founder never updated.

- **Articulate (A)**: They walked the founder

through how they cobbled the info together, referencing an outdated document.

- **Study (S)**: The founder realized he never told anyone how he picks key metrics. The junior guessed half of them.

- **Easier (E)**: The junior found sorting and formatting the data trivially easy—an area the founder always hated.

Outcome

The junior ended up standardizing half the process in a single day, saving both of them hours. Next cycle, they refined the metrics with the founder's input. Within a month, the founder was completely out of "data report mode," freeing him for bigger strategic moves.

The HR Onboarding Overhaul

Scenario

- **Task**: Updating the internal onboarding manual for new hires.
- **Handoff**: The founder had always done it himself, believing "nobody knows the culture better."
- **Triad Approval**: "That's a perfect internal project—high impact, repeated often, but not front-facing."

First C.a.s.e. Meeting

- **Challenges (C)**: The employee discovered contradictory instructions from old versions. They weren't sure which to keep.
- **Articulate (A)**: Step by step, they showed how they cross-referenced Slack messages, old PDFs,

and random email threads from the founder.
- **Study (S)**: They admitted they had no "north star" about what new hires truly need day one vs. day thirty.
- **Easier (E)**: They found capturing the company's "why we do it this way" surprisingly straightforward because the founder had talked about it in all-hands meetings. They just typed it up.

Outcome

The updated manual was far more coherent than the founder's old patchwork. The employee recommended changes that the founder never considered—like short videos from each department head. Everybody gained clarity. By the second iteration, the founder barely touched the manual at all.

Post C.A.S.E Meeting Debrief

Once the C.A.S.E. Method session wraps up, take a moment to update your triad. Keep it simple. A quick text or a 5-minute voice note is enough to share how it went and keep them engaged. You might reflect on:

- "What was your biggest aha moment?"
- "Did you slip into lecturing or micromanaging?"
- "What's your next iteration going to look like?"

These small check-ins go a long way. Your triad can help spot blind spots and will nudge you to schedule a follow-up session if the task is recurring or if any new challenges arise.

Resist The Urge To "Fix And Forget"

If your triad notices you're not scheduling follow-up C.A.S.E. sessions, they'll call you out:

"How do you know your team member is truly improving if you never revisit it?"

That's the beauty of an accountability triad. They keep you from slipping back into old habits once the "new project excitement" wears off.

LOOKING AHEAD: FAILURES ON THE HORIZON

You've now experienced how the four simple questions of the C.A.S.E. Method can transform a typical feedback session into a powerful transfer of thinking. But there's a deeper level to master: the art of asking follow-up questions that truly excavate understanding.

In the next chapter, we'll explore one of the most underrated leadership skills: the art of crafting powerful follow-up questions.

You'll learn how to:

- Cut through defensiveness
- Spark genuine self-reflection
- Trigger those game-changing *"aha!"* moments

The right question, asked at the right time, can do more than hours of explanation ever could. Turn the page to unlock this next level of leadership—one that turns every conversation into a catalyst for growth.

CHAPTER 7 - *THE ART OF ASKING QUESTIONS THAT TRANSFORM THINKING*

Here's the hard truth: You can't tell someone how to think—at least not if you want them to do it well. If you truly want to develop independent thinkers on your team, you have to guide them to discover how they think for themselves.

And the best way to do that? Ask better questions. Questions are the secret sauce that transforms your people from order-takers into independent thinkers. If you master this chapter, you'll master the difference between pushing tasks onto employees (that's delegation-lite) and actually transferring your genius so they can solve problems like you—but without depending on you.

Chapter 7

ASK BETTER QUESTIONS

Sounds good? Then buckle up. This is where we turn your C.A.S.E. Method from instructions into true innovation on your team.

How Questions Fit into

the C.A.S.E. Method

Recall the four pillars of the C.A.S.E. Method meeting:

1. C – Challenge: "What challenges did you face in completing this task?"
2. A – Articulate: "Walk me through exactly how you did this, step by step."
3. S – Study: "Why did you make those choices, and what guided your thinking?"
4. E – Easier Than Expected: "Which parts came naturally, and why do you think that was?"

These questions form your foundation. But it's critical to understand when to probe deeper and when to simply listen.

For the Challenge (C) and Articulate (A) phases: Your primary job is simple: **shut up and listen**. Ask the initial question, then practice active listening without interruption. This isn't the time for follow-up questions or conversation—it's about gathering raw data about their experience and process. Your silence during these phases is powerful; it creates space for your team member to fully express their challenges and steps without being led in any direction. (NOTE: mind your facial expressions…they speak too)

For the Study (S) phase: Now comes the turning point: the **Study** phase.

This is where transformation happens—and where your questioning skills become essential.

After listening to their story, this is your chance to excavate their thinking. You're not just trying to clarify *what* they did—you're uncovering *why* they did it and *how* they made decisions in real time.

Here are examples of powerful follow-up questions you might ask:

- "What surprised you most about the challenge you mentioned with the timeline?"
- "At step three, when you decided to consult with Marketing, what factors influenced that decision?"
- "You mentioned changing the approach

midway through—what assumptions were you making initially that shifted?"
- "How might this decision have affected other parts of the project?"
- "What principles or values guided this particular choice?"
- "What alternatives did you consider at this critical decision point?"
- "How did you prioritize competing concerns when making this decision?"

The Study phase is where transformation happens. Your questions here should help your team member excavate their own thinking process, uncovering assumptions, values, and decision frameworks they may not have been conscious of using.

For the Easier Than Expected (E) phase: After exploring their thinking deeply, your questions shift to leveraging strengths:

- "How might we leverage this strength in

other areas?"
- "What does this natural ability tell us about your unique perspective?"
- "How could we design future processes to capitalize on this strength?"

The key insight: proper question sequencing matters as much as the questions themselves. First, gather information through listening (C & A), then explore thinking through targeted questions (S), then identify strengths and future applications (E).

Why Better Questions Drive Better Thinking

The "Judger" Vs. "Learner" Mindset

Marilee Adams wrote an entire book, *Change Your Questions, Change Your Life*, showing that when we operate in what she calls a "Judger Mindset," we ask questions like "Why didn't you do this the way I said?" or "What's wrong with you people?" Those aren't questions—they're accusations. They shut your team down faster than a power outage.

In contrast, a "Learner Mindset" explores possibilities. It asks, "What can we discover here?" or "Help me understand how you arrived at that choice." Notice the difference? In one scenario, your people clam up, give you safe answers, and vow never to step out of line again. On the other hand, they open up, share the real story, and learn to solve problems at a higher-level next time.

Stat to Chew On: A 2023 study published in *Harvard Business Review* found that when managers use open-ended, curiosity-driven questions in one-on-one meetings, team problem-solving scores improved by **47%**.

THE DELEGATION TRAP

Why Your Old Approach Doesn't Work

- **Telling** someone the answer? They might get it done once, but they'll never truly own the process.
- **Asking** them the right question? That's a game changer. They become the answer—they internalize the method behind it. That means next time, they won't be banging on your door

at 10 p.m. for directions.

Think about your own growth. You didn't become a decision-making machine overnight. You learned by stumbling, experimenting, and questioning. So if you want your team to replicate (or even better) your thinking, you've got to let them do the same. And that starts with asking better questions.

How Questions Fit into the C.A.S.E. Method

Recall the four pillars of the C.A.S.E. Method meeting:

1. **C – Challenge**: "What challenges did you face completing this task?"
2. **A – Articulate**: "Walk me through exactly how you did this, step by step."
3. **S – Study**: "Why did you make those choices, and what guided your thinking?"
4. **E – Easier Than Expected**: "Which parts came naturally, and why do you think that was?"

These aren't just routine check-ins—they're structured opportunities to think, reflect, and grow. But here's the catch: if you stop at surface-level answers, you'll miss the goldmine. If you want innovation, insight, and independence, you need to *go deeper*.

Here's where we weave in new, *transformational* questions—ones that spark creativity, help them confront flawed assumptions, and reveal blind spots.

These questions turn your C.A.S.E. meeting from a "follow-my-steps" lecture into a two-way exploration of why certain decisions were made.

Shifting from Accusation to Curiosity

Let's be honest: we've all said things that shut down conversations. Take a look at these common phrases—and how to flip them into curiosity-driven questions:

Old Way (Judger Mindset)	New Way (Learner Mindset)
"Why on earth would you do it that way?"	"I see you tried a different approach. Could you walk me through what led you there?"
"You know we always use Tool A, right? Why didn't you just do that?"	"What made you decide Tool B was the best option? What advantages did you see?"

"I guess I'll fix it. Next time, pay attention."	"What's one thing you'd do differently if you had more clarity from the start? How can we ensure that clarity next time?"
"Well, in my experience, that's not how it's done. Let's just do it my way."	"It sounds like you tried something new. Could you walk me through what you discovered and how we might refine our approach?"
"I appreciate the effort, but next time, let's do it the right way, okay?"	"I'm curious about your approach. What if we compare your method and our usual method to see the best elements of both?"
"It's obviously simpler to do it my way, but let's see what you did."	"Tell me about your thought process behind this alternative approach—I'd love to see if it might improve our standard."

Notice how the second versions open up the conversation rather than shutting it down. According to *Change Your Questions, Change Your Life*, the questions we ask determine the quality of thinking we get back—and by extension, the results our team produces.

Transformational Questioning in Action

Let's see how questioning transforms a real delegation situation. Imagine Elena, a marketing director, discussing a campaign rollout with Jamal, who has taken over this responsibility.

Ineffective Question Approach:

Elena: "Did you get approval from Legal before launching the campaign?"

Jamal: "No, I didn't think we needed to since it was similar to our last campaign."

Elena: "You always need to check with Legal. That's our policy."

Jamal: "Sorry, I didn't know that was mandatory for every campaign."

Elena: "Well, now you know. Make sure you do it next time."

This exchange provides information, but no growth in thinking. Elena is telling, not developing judgment.

Effective C.A.S.E. Question Progression:

During the Articulate phase (simply listening):

Elena: "Walk me through your approval process before the campaign went live."

Jamal: "I got approvals from Product and Brand, but not Legal since this campaign was so similar to our last one, which Legal had already approved."

(Elena takes notes but doesn't interrupt or ask follow-ups yet)

During the Study phase (exploring thinking):

Elena: "What factors did you consider when deciding whether Legal needed to review this campaign?"

Jamal: "I guess I was thinking about whether there were new claims or offers that hadn't been vetted before."

Elena: "That's a good starting point. What might be some risks of not getting Legal's approval even on similar campaigns?"

Jamal: "I suppose regulations might have changed, or small differences I didn't notice could have legal implications."

Elena: "How might those risks impact other teams or our company's position?"

Jamal: "If we made claims that weren't properly vetted, we could face compliance issues or mislead customers, which could damage our reputation and create problems for Customer Service."

Transitioning to solutions:

Elena: "Given what we've discussed, how might you approach this decision differently next time?"

Jamal: "I should probably create a decision tree for when Legal approval is mandatory versus optional. Would you mind reviewing that with me once I draft it?"

Notice how Elena never simply told Jamal what to do. Through carefully sequenced questions during the Study phase—after gathering information in the Articulate phase—she helped him discover the principles behind the policy. Next time, he won't just blindly follow a rule—he'll understand the reasoning and apply good judgment.

Examples of Transformational Questions

You already have four anchors in the C.A.S.E. structure. Now let's add a layer of "booster questions" to help your team see beyond the obvious.

Reframing Questions

"If we approached this from the client's perspective, how would it look?"

- *When to Use:* If your team only sees the internal steps, but you want them to consider the client experience.
- *Outcome:* They begin to weigh decisions

differently, factoring in user impact, brand reputation, and bigger-picture goals.

Probing Assumptions

"What assumptions did you make that led you to this path?"

- *When to Use:* Whenever you sense a team member is glossing over hidden beliefs.
- *Outcome:* They learn to question their own assumptions, which is critical for creative problem-solving.

Future-Pacing

"If we repeated this task six months from now, what would you do differently from the start?"

- *When to Use:* After they've explained how they tackled the job.
- *Outcome:* They immediately shift to a continuous-improvement mindset.

Encouraging Self-Evaluation

"How did this result match the vision you initially had? Where did it diverge?"

- *When to Use:* Right after they complete the task.
- *Outcome:* They compare outcomes vs. intentions, learning to self-correct.

Curiosity Over Judgment

"What other options did you consider—and why did you choose this one?"

- *When to Use:* If you want to see how thoroughly they explored alternatives.
- *Outcome:* They realize leadership wants them to weigh different angles, not just take the quickest fix.

A **2024 Deloitte survey** found that teams who embraced *choice exploration* reported **29% higher first-attempt problem resolution**. That's not fluff—that's real leverage. Imagine 29% fewer issues landing on your desk because your team learned to think for themselves.

This is the power of question-based leadership. It's how you step out of the micromanager's chair and into the role of a true multiplier.

When Questions Meet Resistance

Even the most artfully framed questions sometimes encounter defensive reactions. People have been conditioned to view questions from leaders as judgments or tests, not opportunities for growth.

Here's how to navigate that resistance:

1. Acknowledge And Normalize

If you sense defensiveness, address it directly:

"I notice this might feel like an interrogation, but I'm genuinely curious about your thinking process here. There's no right or wrong answer—I want to understand your perspective."

2. Reframe From Personal To Process

If questions about their decisions feel too personal, shift the focus from *them* to the *process*:

Instead of: "Why did you choose this approach?"
Try: "What does this approach offer that alternatives might not?"

3. Use The Third-Person Technique

Sometimes removing the "you" helps reduce perceived criticism:

Instead of: "What concerns did you have about this approach?"
Try: "What concerns might someone have when evaluating this approach?"

4. The Backup Question Strategy

Not every question lands on the first try. That's okay. Have alternative phrasings ready when your first question doesn't generate insight:

If "What factors influenced this decision?" yields a surface response, try:

"If you were coaching someone else facing this exact situation, what would you advise them to consider?"

5. The Silence Tool

Perhaps the most powerful technique is simply waiting. When you ask a thought-provoking question, resist the urge to fill the silence. Count to ten silently if needed. Most people will fill the gap with deeper reflection if you give them time to think.

Remember: The goal isn't to force insights but to create a space where reflection can happen naturally. Sometimes the most powerful question is followed by your most disciplined silence.

Tone & Delivery: It's Not Just What You Ask, But How

Your words carry weight. But your *tone*? That's what your team will feel. If you sound annoyed, rushed, or condescending, it won't matter if your question is gold—your employee will shut down. They'll slip into defensive mode, and you'll lose the chance to transform them into an independent thinker.

- **Slow Down:** Give them space to formulate answers. If you cut them off, they'll give short, safe responses.
- **Stay Neutral:** Body language—like an eye-roll—speaks louder than a 300-page SOP.
- **Acknowledge Wins & Insights:** If they do something well, say it. You want to reinforce that you value their perspective.

Brené Brown says, "Clarity is kindness." In questions,

clarity means showing you're here to learn, not to punish.

When Teaching Becomes Inevitable: How to Insert Guidance Gracefully

Yes, there will be moments when teaching is unavoidable. Maybe they're missing a key concept, or they're stuck.

That's okay—but *don't jump in too soon.*

First, ask enough questions to understand where the gap really is. Then, when you do offer insight, weave it in gently.

> "If you had this extra piece of data, how might that have changed your approach? Let me show you a rule of thumb we use here."

That's not "lecturing"—that's guiding them to see the

principle in action. You're weaving in your expertise but leaving them space to connect the dots.

Coaching Mindset: "It's Not About Me Telling You—It's About You Discovering"

Leaders who adopt a coaching approach see exponential growth in team autonomy. The **International Coaching Federation** data suggests that organizations implementing a coaching style see a **70%** improvement in overall team performance within the first year.

Think of it like teaching someone to drive:

- You could bark instructions from the passenger seat.
- Or you could ask, "Why do you think shifting now matters? What's happening with the engine's RPMs?"

The second approach makes them *feel* the car's rhythm,

so they develop real skills. Once they do, they can drive anywhere, not just the same route you taught.

Closing Thoughts: The Questions You Ask Today Become the Team You Lead Tomorrow

With these questioning techniques, you've now mastered the art of drawing out your team's thinking rather than imposing your own. But there's another critical piece of the delegation puzzle we haven't addressed: how to handle the inevitable moments when things go wrong.

In Chapter 8, we'll explore why failure isn't just an acceptable part of the C.A.S.E. Method—it's essential fuel for growth. You'll discover how to transform mistakes from sources of frustration into powerful learning moments that actually accelerate your team's development. Turn the page to see why the most successful delegation systems don't avoid failure—they harness it.

CHAPTER 8 - *LEARNING FROM FAILURE—WHY THE C.A.S.E. METHOD WORKS EVEN WHEN THINGS GO WRONG*

Failure Isn't Fatal—It's Fuel!

If you've followed the previous chapters, you know by now that the C.A.S.E. Method is all about turning your team into independent, resourceful thinkers—so you can finally step away from micromanaging. But there's a big, gnarly question still lurking:

"What happens when they fail?"

Let's get real. Failure—that gut-punch moment when your carefully delegated project goes off the rails, or your star employee butchers a client pitch—often feels like the end of the world. As entrepreneurs and founders, we spend years building a zero-mistake culture (often unintentionally). We lurk over shoulders or step in to "save" the day, rationalizing it as "maintaining quality." But ironically, that fear of failure is exactly what keeps us trapped in the Founder's Trap.

In this chapter, we're going to rip that Band-Aid right off. We'll see why letting your team make mistakes —and even fail spectacularly—is not just acceptable, but essential to the C.A.S.E. Method. And by the time you finish reading, you'll walk away convinced that "failure" is your most powerful tool for building a bulletproof, self-sustaining business.

So buckle up. This chapter might sting a bit. But I promise, if you embrace these truths about failure, you'll open the door to exponential growth—for your team, your business, and, yes, even you.

WHAT MOST FOUNDERS GET WRONG ABOUT FAILURE

The Myth of the One-Shot Success

We entrepreneurs love neat success stories: "He delegated the marketing campaign once, and the team executed perfectly." Or "She hired the perfect sales VP and the company 10x'ed overnight." It's the highlight-reel version of delegation that pops up in motivational LinkedIn posts—but it's not reality.

In reality, the path to effective delegation is riddled with bad calls, messed-up presentations, near-missed deadlines, code fiascos, and client issues. When we see top-tier companies that scale beyond their founders' personal capacity, it's not because they avoided failure—it's because they learned how to harness it.

A 2024 study in the Harvard Business Review found that companies with a healthy tolerance for employee-driven failure (paired with structured post-mortems) were 31% more likely to achieve year-over-year growth in new product launches. In other words, the biggest leaps in innovation happen when you turn flops into fuel. If you avoid or bury every mistake, you bury your company's ability to learn.

Why "No-Failure" Cultures Breed Bottlenecks

Maybe you've said this out loud—or at least thought it:

"We can't afford big mistakes right now."

Trust me, I've been there. But the more you push for error-free execution, the more you force your team to either:

1. Hide mistakes (which leads to bigger blowups later), or
2. Rely on you for every micro-decision.

Recent Gallup research (2023) backs this up: Organizations with *zero tolerance for failure* experience the **highest turnover among top talent**. Why? Because high performers want room to experiment, make judgment calls, and think creatively.

Kill that freedom, and you kill their motivation. What's left? A team that either coasts through the motions or constantly looks over their shoulder, waiting for your approval.

And you? You're left answering Slack messages at 11 p.m., approving color schemes for landing pages, and "vacationing" with your laptop. Your weekends vanish under a mountain of "urgent" tasks. And that dream of stepping away for a real vacation? Kiss it goodbye.

WHY FAILURE MATTERS IN THE C.A.S.E. METHOD

Recall the four pillars of the C.A.S.E. Method:

C – Challenge: "What challenges did you face in completing this task?" A – Articulate: "Walk me through, step by step, exactly how you completed this task." S – Study: "Why did you make those choices, and what guided your thinking?" E – Easier Than Expected: "What parts came naturally to you, and why?"

When your team completes a delegated task, and it doesn't go as planned, that is where the C.A.S.E. Method shines. Because it transforms "failure" into:

1. Data: Raw information about how your team thinks.
2. Coaching Material: A blueprint for clarifying your approach.
3. Team Empowerment: A shared sense of discovery that fosters trust and independence.

Instead of you swooping in to fix everything or tear them down, you use the C.A.S.E. meeting to dissect the missteps, identify the mental gaps, and refine both your team's thinking and your process. The fiasco you dreaded? It becomes a teachable moment with massive ROI.

Key Insight

The question isn't, "How do I prevent failure?" It's "How do I handle failure so we learn faster?"

The Vicious Cycle vs. The Virtuous Cycle

- **Vicious Cycle**: Founder sees a mistake → Founder freaks out → Founder takes the task back → Team confidence plummets → Founder remains the bottleneck.

- **Virtuous Cycle**: Team stumbles → Founder calmly triggers a C.A.S.E. meeting → We glean insights from mistakes → Team confidence grows → Founder delegates more, not less.

This is the crucial pivot. If you yank tasks back at the first sign of trouble, you reaffirm the unspoken lie: "Only I can do this." But if you lean in and say, "Great, let's see what we can learn," you dismantle that cage you built around yourself (and your team).

THE RESEARCH & STUDIES BEHIND PRODUCTIVE FAILURE

This isn't just motivational talk—there's a growing body of research that shows how "failing forward" can be systematically leveraged to build stronger teams and better systems.

1. Stanford Graduate School of Business (2022)

Explored 214 mid-sized companies and found that leaders who encouraged trial-and-error problem-solving — paired with structured feedback sessions) – saw a 45% improvement in employee decision-making autonomy over 12 months.

Key takeaway: The presence of a consistent reflection process—like C.A.S.E. Method meetings—creates psychological "safe zones" that empower teams to own their missteps and fix them internally.

2. Massachusetts Institute of Technology (MIT) Sloan Study (2023)

This study focused on knowledge-intensive companies (consulting firms, tech startups, R&D labs) and found that repeated "mini-failures"—like failed pilot tests—**led to faster breakthroughs** when accompanied by structured debriefs.

Core insight: The key difference between companies that benefited from failure and those that didn't? Leadership's willingness to **invite open analysis** of mistakes.

3. Journal of Organizational Behavior (2024)

Analyzed over 600 managerial teams across various industries. Found that teams using "failure retrospectives" at least once a month had 36% fewer repeated errors. Specifically cited the practice of "guided self-diagnosis," which is exactly what the S (Study) portion of C.A.S.E. fosters: employees unraveling why they did what they did.

Put simply, failure plus structure equals growth. If you need permission from science to loosen your white-knuckle grip on perfection, there it is.

THE COURAGE TO LET TEAM MEMBERS FAIL

Real-World Example: The Marketing Catastrophe That Became a Masterclass

Let me tell you about Alisha, a client I coached who ran a thriving online marketing agency. Her biggest fear was letting an employee handle a crucial client's rebranding campaign—one that had serious revenue implications. But she was drowning in her own workload, so we decided to push that fear aside and delegate anyway.

Week 1: Alisha handed the entire account strategy to her top project manager, Daryl.

Week 2: The client's new brand guidelines launched with major fanfare. Daryl was proud, Alisha was biting her nails.

Week 3: Everything imploded. The rebranding contained an unfortunate phrase that triggered a backlash from the client's bilingual audience. This had the potential to be a PR meltdown.

Alisha's gut reaction?

"I knew it. I should never have delegated this. Now I have to fix it!"

But with a nudge from her accountability partner, she paused. Instead of jumping in to clean up the mess, she pulled Daryl into a **C.A.S.E. Method meeting**. Here's how it unfolded:

- **Challenge (C):** Daryl revealed he never verified the phrase with a bilingual colleague because he assumed it was "fine." The real challenge was time pressure and a lack of cultural checks.

- **Articulate (A):** Step by step, Daryl described how he found the tagline, how he tested it, and how he green-lit the final version.

- **Study (S):** Together, they realized Daryl had focused so much on visual elements that he missed linguistic nuance. Alisha also realized she'd never shared her personal language-vetting process—something she usually did herself.

- **Easier Than Expected (E):** Daryl breezed through color palette alignment—something that always took Alisha hours. This was a hidden strength that Daryl possessed, meaning he should handle more design tasks in the future.

The meltdown was resolved (yes, it was messy for a few days), but the outcome? Daryl's new system for cross-checking brand copy across languages was better than anything Alisha had used before. The client saw them scramble and fix it in record time—and ended up praising them for the comeback. The relationship deepened. Alisha began trusting Daryl with bigger responsibilities.

Would that have happened if Alisha had just yanked

the entire project back at the first sign of failure? No chance. She would have missed the insight that Daryl was a powerhouse in design alignment. She never would've built out that improved language vetting system.

BETTER QUESTIONS FOR HARD TIMES

Remember back in Chapter 7 when we explored the power of asking better questions? That skill becomes even more critical when you're facing failure.

When things fall apart and your instincts scream, *"I need to fix this now!"*, pause. Instead of reacting or assigning blame, turn to your question-asking toolbox. The right question can turn disaster into discovery.

Try these:

- **"Help me understand what led you to that decision?"**

- **"What assumptions were you making here, and why?"**

- **"If you could rewind time, what would you do differently—starting right now?"**

Yes, it can feel awkward to slow down in the midst of a crash. But that's precisely the moment when curiosity pays dividends. If you can transform that tension into a constructive dialogue—rather than a blame session—you're showing your team that mistakes are a stepping stone, not a tombstone.

Why does this matter so much? Because in times of failure, your team is braced for impact. They expect you to swoop in with anger, micromanaging, or "I told you so" energy. But when you come in with clarifying questions that are designed to help them reflect, something remarkable happens:

- **They trust you more** because you're not here to punish but to understand.

- **They learn faster** because they have to articulate and analyze their own missteps.

- **They become proactive** about preventing similar failures in the future.

Essentially, better questions become your life raft in the middle of a storm. They guide you from "We messed up" to "We learned something vital." And that is how you transform short-term loss into long-term gain.

So the next time you feel the panic rising—ask yourself, "Which question can unlock growth here?" Because the right question is always a bridge to a better outcome.

TURNING FAILURES INTO FUEL: THE SYSTEMATIC APPROACH

Now that you see the value of "productive failure," let's ground it in a clear, step-by-step approach. By combining C.A.S.E. with an explicit failure-handling protocol, you'll systematically build resilience into your delegation process.

1. Set the Stage

- In the kickoff: Let your team know from Day One that mistakes are expected, not punished.

- Clarify that the real "failure" is hiding errors or refusing to learn from them.

2. Allow the Mistake to Happen (Without Rescue)
- We've hammered this point. Stop diving in to "fix" issues prematurely.
- If the house is on fire, sure, intervene—but for

recoverable mistakes, let them unfold. That's how you get raw data.

3. Conduct the C.A.S.E. Meeting
- Use the four questions to dissect the aftermath.
- Remember to lead with curiosity, not condemnation. If you jump into "What were you thinking?" territory, you'll poison the well.

4. Collaborate on Corrections
- Don't just highlight what went wrong—co-create the solution.
- "Given what we've learned, how should we handle this next time?"
- Document the new steps in your updated SOP or team wiki so no one repeats the same error.

5. Celebrate the Lesson
- Even if it was costly or time-consuming, find a way to appreciate the new insights.
- This doesn't mean cheering about messing up

a client's account, but it does mean saying, "I'm proud we uncovered a gap in our process and fixed it."

6. Iterate

- Keep repeating C.A.S.E. for subsequent tasks or new attempts.

- Over time, your "failure rate" might not even go down—because you'll be taking bigger risks. But your "learning velocity" will skyrocket.

"But What If My Clients See The Failure?"

Welcome to the real world, friend. Clients might see a slip-up. That's part of building a team. But clients—and customers at large—judge you more on how you respond than on whether a mistake happened. Show them your ability to adapt and fix issues quickly, and many will admire your resilience. It's also how you quietly position your business as one that invests in long-term growth and continuous improvement.

That's how you build not just stronger teams—but a stronger

reputation, too.

HOW TO HANDLE THE BIGGEST FEARS AROUND FAILURE

Let's talk about the emotional friction—because people aren't robots. Your team might be terrified of messing up. You might be terrified it'll cost you a major client or a big chunk of revenue. The only way to transform that fear is to name it and handle it directly.

Fear #1: "We'll lose customers or tarnish our brand."

Response:

• Start with micro-delegations for high-stakes tasks. High-stakes tasks benefit from micro-delegations first. If an employee can handle 80% of the puzzle, you step in for the final 20%—but in a coach's role, not as a rescuer.

• Over time, you reduce your 20% to 10%, then 5%,

until your oversight is minimal.

Fear #2: "I'll look incompetent as a leader if my team messes up."

Response:

• This is an ego trap. Great leaders do not appear incompetent—they appear courageous, transparent and growth-minded.

• A 2023 survey by the Global Leadership Institute found that 71% of employees trust leaders more when they see them handling mistakes openly and calmly.

• In other words, your brand as a leader improves when you support your team, not hide their mistakes.

Fear #3: "Isn't it faster if I just fix the mistakes myself?"

Response:

• Maybe. The first time. But what about the 50th time? Over months and years, the "quick fix" drains hundreds of hours from you.

- Short-term speed vs. long-term freedom: Which would you prefer?

- According to a 2024 Deloitte study, leaders who delegate decision-making early see a 38% faster climb in revenue over five years. The difference is that their people develop independence quickly instead of perpetually waiting on the boss.

FAILURE ON PURPOSE— HOW TO CREATE LOW-STAKES LEARNING LABS

Sometimes the smartest move is to design safe, intentional spaces for failure. It may sound counterintuitive, but creating internal "learning labs" helps your team make mistakes in a controlled environment—where the impact is small, but the lessons are real.

Example: The Pilot Program Approach

• Step 1: Identify a new product feature or marketing experiment with medium priority.

• Step 2: Delegate it fully to a capable team member (or small group).

• Step 3: Impose a short timeline, so they have to think on their feet.

• Step 4: Let them launch, present, or test it with a subset of real customers.

• Step 5: If it bombs, run the C.A.S.E. Method meeting. If it soars, also run the C.A.S.E. Method meeting to dissect what worked.

By narrowing the scope—like limiting exposure to 10% of your customer base—you contain the risk while giving your team a real-world opportunity to experiment, learn, and grow.

Over time, you can launch multiple small-scale pilots. Each one becomes a "failure lab" or "success lab"— a space to stretch, stumble, and strengthen. The principle is simple: create real consequences, but minimize permanent harm.

FAILURE AND COMPANY CULTURE —TACKLING THE MINDSET SHIFT

If your entire company is used to you (the founder) stepping in, then you probably have a culture where failure is taboo. Reversing that culture starts with publicly celebrating the process of learning from mistakes.

1. **Company-Wide "Lesson of the Month"**
   - Encourage each department to nominate a "lesson

of the month," which might be the biggest mistake that provided the biggest insight.

- Present it in a short, positive way at your monthly all-hands. No blame. Just outcomes and improvements.

2. **"Fail-Fest" Workshops**

- Borrowing from the tradition of "fail-cons" in Silicon Valley, host an internal workshop once or twice a year where each team highlights one big flop —and how they turned it around.

- It feels silly at first. But watch how it normalizes open discussion of errors.

3. **Founder Vulnerability**

- If you can't admit your own missteps, why should your team?

- When you lead by example—saying, "I botched that decision last quarter. Here's what I learned"—you give permission for everyone else to own theirs.

A 2025 Brené Brown Leadership survey found

that 82% of employees in "high-vulnerability" leadership environments reported stronger personal accountability and lower fear of failure.

In other words, when leaders openly admit they don't have all the answers, the entire organization breathes easier—and learns faster.

REAL-LIFE FAILURE STORIES +
THE C.A.S.E. TURNAROUND

We can talk theory all day, but let's bring in more real-world narratives to hammer this home.

1. The Start-Up CFO Catastrophe

• Scenario: A newly hired CFO invests a chunk of cash in a complicated currency hedge. It backfires, costing the company tens of thousands of dollars.

• Usual Founder Reaction: Rage or panic, followed by demoting or firing the CFO.

• C.A.S.E. Reaction:

Challenge: The CFO explains that confusion about the founder's growth plans led him to hedge a currency risk that never materialized.

Articulate: Step by step, he shares the formula he used and the assumptions about incoming foreign revenue.

Study: They realize the founder never clarified the pivot to local markets, so the CFO was operating with outdated data.

Easier: The CFO found daily forecasting easy but never thought to confirm assumptions with the founder.

Outcome

The CFO reworks the capital management strategy and establishes recurring check-ins. The founder learns to share strategic pivots the moment they happen. Losses are recovered within three months—and a new capital oversight system is born.

2. The Social Media Intern's Viral Gaffe

• Scenario: A well-meaning intern schedules a flurry of tweets with a joke that's misread as offensive.

• Panic: The brand's mentions blow up, negative sentiments swirl, leadership freaks out.

• C.A.S.E. Approach:

Challenge: The intern confesses she felt rushed to fill the social calendar, never ran the joke by anyone else.

Articulate: She outlines her full process—revealing she mimicked a competitor's comedic style without knowing the brand's tone guidelines.

Study: They discover the brand guidelines are outdated and missing any references to "approved comedic tone." The entire social team had zero clarity on what was off-limits.

Easier: The intern found scheduling tools intuitive and finished them faster than the old social media manager ever did.

Outcome

The team creates a brand voice style guide. The intern (still employed, by the way) ends up teaching the rest of the team how to schedule content faster. The brand recovers by issuing a sincere apology and capitalizes on the PR moment to show a commitment to inclusive humor.

In both cases, the crisis wasn't the end. It became the catalyst for better systems, stronger communication, and long-term growth. The founder's job was to hold the line: "We will not bury this. We will talk it out. We will learn. And we will be stronger on the other side."

ACTION STEPS TO EMBRACE FAILURE AS FUEL

We're not just talking concepts here. Let's get tactical. Grab your C.A.S.E. Method Workbook (or a notepad if you're old school) and walk through these steps.

1. Declare Failure Part of the Deal

- At your next team meeting, openly state: "We learn by doing, and that includes messing up. Let's all commit to using C.A.S.E. to dissect and improve whenever that happens."

2. Pick a Low-Risk Experiment

• Choose a project (internal or external) that you can safely afford to let your team handle with minimal supervision. Let them figure it out.

3. Plan the Next C.A.S.E. Method Meeting Beforehand

• The moment you delegate, set the follow-up *before* they begin. Whether it flops or flies, you'll have a dedicated space to review what happened and why.

4. Document the Lesson

• Update your SOPs or internal knowledge base. Make sure the improvement is official, not just a conversation in your Slack channel that's forgotten tomorrow.

5. Reward the Learning

- If someone flags a big error, or shares how they messed up, give them props for bringing it to light. When you reward honesty and improvement, you create a culture where it's safe to share missteps.

6. Check in with Your Accountability Partner/Triad

- Tell them about the slip-ups. Let them challenge you on whether you jumped in too soon. Use them to keep you honest about letting your team own the outcome. You should let them hold you to your own standards.

YOUR NEXT MOVE—DO YOU RETREAT OR ADVANCE?

Right now, you have a choice:

Option 1: Retreat

Tighten your grip, revert to perfectionism, continue rewriting your team's deliverables, and watch your freedom slip away day by day.

Option 2: Advance

Let them fail (within reason). Use C.A.S.E. to dissect the wreckage, glean the gold, and refine your processes. Witness your employees take ownership, grow in confidence, and handle bigger tasks with less of your input.

I know which path you want to choose. After all, you picked up (or listened to) a book that's dedicated to busting you out of the Founder's Trap. Embracing failure is the hinge that will swing that door wide open.

As Winston Churchill famously said, "Success is stumbling from failure to failure with no loss of enthusiasm." That isn't just a witty line—it's a blueprint for unstoppable progress. Because every "stumble" is data, and data fuels better decisions next time.

A GUT-CHECK BEFORE YOU CLOSE THIS CHAPTER

Before you move on, take a moment for one final exercise—a quick internal C.A.S.E. Method meeting with yourself. This isn't busy work. It's a vital pulse check to reveal what might still be holding you back.

1. **C (Challenge):**

Ask Yourself: "What's my biggest fear about letting my team fail?" Write it Down: Spell out the worst-case scenario. Is it losing clients, public embarrassment, or wasted money?

2. **A (Articulate):**

Ask Yourself: "What am I currently doing to either prevent or hide that fear?" Reflection: Maybe you're doubling up on meetings, or rewriting proposals at 2 a.m.

3. **S (Study):**

Ask Yourself: "Why do I believe I'm the only one who can prevent this worst-case scenario?"

Dig Deeper: Is it your ego? A belief that no one else cares as much as you? A team that hasn't been trained to step up yet? Identify the root belief.

4. **E (Easier Than Expected):**

Ask Yourself: "What part of letting go might actually feel like a relief once I do it?"

Revelation: Perhaps you'll discover you hate a certain task more than you realized, or your team is better at it anyway.

How did that feel? A little uncomfortable? Probably. But that tension—that mix of fear and possibility—is exactly where transformation begins. If you're serious about building a self-sustaining business, this is the threshold you need to cross.

FINAL THOUGHTS: FAILURE AS THE FAST TRACK TO FREEDOM

Look, I won't sugarcoat it: letting your team fail will pinch your pride. It might pinch your wallet here or there. But compared to the cost of remaining the sole genius in your company, it's a bargain. Because every failure, when used wisely, becomes a stepping stone. Your team gets sharper. Your systems get smarter. Your business becomes stronger.

You didn't start this journey to stay chained to your inbox or to babysit every project. You started it for *freedom*, *scale*, *impact*—or maybe just a full night's sleep. And the only way to reach any of that is with a capable, thinking team. One that can carry the load without you constantly steering the ship. And you don't get a robust team by coddling them or punishing every blunder. You get it by harnessing those stumbles as stepping stones.

So here's my challenge to you:

Go fail.

Delegating that "too-important" project? Do it this month. Assign that campaign to the green team member who's never done one before.
Let them wrestle with it—just a bit—and then bring them into a C.A.S.E. Method debrief.

Watch what happens.

You'll start to see so-called "disasters" morph into data-rich breakthroughs. You'll see your team rise to the challenge, take ownership, and begin to outpace your expectations. You'll feel your own grip loosen—and your capacity to lead expand.

Because every time you step back, your team steps up.

That's the real magic of the C.A.S.E. Method—it transforms your personal genius into a shared, ever-evolving system that no single failure can derail. With each iteration, your business gets stronger, your team gets smarter, and you become the kind of leader who can walk away for a week—or a month—confident that progress doesn't stop when you leave the room.

And next, you'll see exactly how to spread this culture of iterative, unstoppable improvement across your entire organization. Chapter 9 will show you the blueprint for scaling the C.A.S.E. Method so every manager, every department, and eventually every project can leverage the same approach—leaving you free to explore even bigger horizons.

Remember: If you're not failing, you're not learning—and if you're not learning, you're not growing. So choose growth. Choose freedom. And choose to let your business breathe, fail, recover, and flourish without you controlling every last detail.

CHAPTER 9 - *SCALING YOUR DELEGATION BEYOND YOURSELF: TRAINING THE TRAINERS*

"If your business can thrive without you sitting in the driver's seat, you've achieved real freedom. Now, the question is: How do you make that freedom last?"

Welcome to the Big Leagues of Delegation

It's time to scale your delegation beyond yourself. In this next phase, your managers—not you—will shoulder the front-line responsibility of teaching, guiding, and correcting your growing team. In other words, you're handing over the baton of "Chief Delegation Mentor" to the folks who are also in the trenches of leadership with you. That's the difference between a business that depends solely on your brilliance, and a business that systematically reproduces your brilliance in others—even when you're not in the room.

If that idea makes you tense, breathe. This is exactly how you escape the founder's trap for good. And in this chapter, you'll learn precisely how to do it—by having your managers **shadow** you running a C.A.S.E. conversation, then gradually step into that conversation themselves, and ultimately run the entire process. Your role? Observe and evaluate how they apply the C.A.S.E. Method with their own team.

It's C.A.S.E. Method all the way down.

How do I know I'm ready to

scale the C.A.S.E Method?

You're ready if you've been using the C.A.S.E. Method consistently for at least six months, across multiple departments, with different team members. You've witnessed the messy, glorious dance between "letting go" and "holding on." You've seen employees stumble—then find their footing and deliver results that might've surprised you. You've stepped into your role as a coach more than a savior, using C.A.S.E. to transform doers into thinkers.

Step 1: Identify the Right Manager(s) to Train

Before you scale, you need to choose who will learn the C.A.S.E. Method from you. Because not every manager is a fit on Day One.

Key Criteria

1. **They Have the Bandwidth** – This next level of leadership can't be so swamped that they're ignoring texts from family. They need mental space to coach someone else.
2. **They Want Real Autonomy** – Some managers quietly love that you're the final "firefighter." They avoid stepping up. You want someone who genuinely wants more ownership.
3. **They Show Potential in Asking Good Questions** – This manager doesn't jump straight to "Let me fix it." Instead, they're at least halfway comfortable letting team members discover solutions.

Action: Take a moment right now and physically **write down the name** of the manager you've chosen in your C.A.S.E. workbook. Then, share your choice with your **Escape the Cage triad**—discuss why you selected that person and what your next steps will be in getting them ready.

If you're struggling to find that perfect person, pick the closest fit. Remember, half of leadership is learned on the job.

Step 2: Shadow the C.A.S.E. Process in Real Time

You've probably run a dozen or more C.A.S.E. Method meetings by now. But to your managers, though, this might still feel abstract. They've heard you talk about it. They might've sat in a meeting or two—but they haven't *really* dissected your approach. So we need to do with them exactly what you did with your employees months ago: let them **shadow** you.

The Three-Stage Shadow Strategy

1. **Stage One: Manager Watches, Takes Notes**

- **Scenario**: You, the owner, help a team member using the C.A.S.E. Method.
- The manager's role is purely observational—pen, paper, and open mind.
- After the meeting, you two hold a quick

debrief: "What did you notice about how I asked questions? Where did I keep quiet and let them squirm?"

2. **Stage Two: Manager Co-Leads**

- **Scenario**: You and the manager **co-run** a C.A.S.E. discussion with the employee.
- The manager takes the lead on the "C" (Challenges) and "E" (Easier Than Expected) questions, while you handle "A" (Articulate) and "S" (Study)—or vice versa.
- Afterward, you exchange feedback: "Why did you choose to phrase that question like that? How did the team member respond?"

3. **Stage Three: Manager Takes Over**

- **Scenario**: The manager runs the C.A.S.E. meeting from start to finish. You're a silent observer (or quietly taking notes).
- After they finish, you hold your own C.A.S.E. evaluation with them. In other words, you ask:

- **C**: "What challenges did *you* face running the meeting?"
- **A**: "Walk me through how you prepared and led this conversation."
- **S**: "Why did you make the choices you did at each stage? How did you handle unexpected questions from the employee?"
- **E**: "Which parts of leading C.A.S.E. came naturally to you, and why do you think that is?"

This final conversation is the meta-layer that cements everything. Now your manager **feels** what it's like to use the C.A.S.E. framework to grow others—and to be evaluated on their own approach.

Step 3: The Owner (You) and Manager Use C.A.S.E. to Evaluate How the Manager Used C.A.S.E.

Let's take a moment to highlight the power in this step:

1. **It Reinforces the Process** – You're not switching to a new set of fancy management frameworks. You're doubling down on the same method, turning it inward on your manager's performance.
2. **It Gives Managers "On the Spot" Experience** – There's no confusion about what "good leadership" means. You literally model the same question-based approach they should use with their direct reports.
3. **It Lets You Catch and Fix Weak Spots Early** – If your manager is too "soft" on certain aspects (e.g., skipping tough follow-up questions), or too controlling (giving solutions instead of guiding), you'll see it in real time. Then you can address it while it's small.

Sample Meta-Conversation

- **You:** "All right, Linda, let's run a C.A.S.E. Method Meeting on your conversation with Jacob."

  1. **C (Challenge):** "What challenges did you face in walking Jacob through that big website migration?"
  2. **A (Articulate):** "Explain how you structured the meeting. Which part did you tackle first, and how did you hand over the floor to him?"
  3. **S (Study):** "Why did you choose to skip asking him about his biggest assumptions? What guided that decision?"
  4. **E (Easier):** "What parts of the meeting came more easily to you than you expected, and why?"

- **Linda:** "I realized I was so worried about hurting Jacob's feelings that I never pushed him to articulate why he repeated the same error. I just jumped in to fix it."

- **You (smiling):** "That's gold. I've been there—guilty as charged. Now, how do we fix that next time?"

Boom. Now Linda's not just a manager; she's an empowered coach who sees the real-time consequences of how she leads. She starts to refine her approach, and you step further back.

Step 4: Gradual Manager Autonomy

Remember how you used to let employees flounder a bit to help them grow? The same principle applies to your managers. They need the wiggle room to "fail" gracefully at leading their own teams, and then correct those mistakes under your guidance—**not** your rescue.

You remain available for:

- High-level strategic insights ("Here's

how I typically approach that departmental challenge").

- Big, business-threatening catastrophes (rare, but it can happen).

But for everyday hiccups, trust your managers' growing leadership muscles. Let them run their own versions of the C.A.S.E. Method with minimal meddling from you. If they bomb, you do a **manager-level** C.A.S.E. meeting after the fact. Next time, they'll do better.

The 90-Day "Manager Incubation" Plan

For those of you who love a bulletproof process, here's a recommended 90-day timeline to train your selected manager(s) in the C.A.S.E. Method:

1. **Weeks 1–2**

    - Manager does "Stage One" shadow on at least two C.A.S.E. sessions you lead.
    - Manager + owner do a quick daily or weekly debrief.

2. **Weeks 3–6**

    - Manager moves to "Stage Two": Co-leading C.A.S.E. with you.
    - You still handle tricky moments, but let them drive.
    - End of Week 6: "Meta" C.A.S.E. with your manager. Ask them to articulate

how they prepared, handled pushback, etc.

3. **Weeks 7–10**
    - Manager tries "Stage Three": Runs an entire C.A.S.E. session solo while you watch silently.
    - You hold a second "meta" meeting to refine their approach.

4. **Weeks 11–12**
    - Manager continues holding regular C.A.S.E. sessions with their direct reports, but you do a monthly check-in to see how it's going.

5. **Weeks 13–16**
    - You gradually step away. Manager is now fully in the driver's seat for departmental delegation.

- You plan to do *another* meta-level C.A.S.E. meeting at the end of Month 4 to ensure everything is on track.

Rinse and repeat for each manager or team lead you want to empower. By the six-month mark, your managers are replicating your leadership style across the board—**without** you chained to the day-to-day.

Common Pitfalls and How to Avoid Them

Let's be real. Delegation at scale sounds great—until the friction hits. Here are some common traps and how to sidestep them:

1. **Pitfall:** "I'm Too Busy to Let Managers Shadow Me."

    - **Reality Check:** If you don't make time to train them, you'll *never* have the time to step away from your business. That's the real "time cost" here.

2. **Pitfall:** Owner Clings to Final Approval on Everything

    - **Fix:** Set clear boundaries for which decisions truly require your sign-off (e.g., legal compliance, major financial investments). Everything else? Let your managers handle it—and course-correct them *after* they try.

3. **Pitfall**: Managers Copy Your Words but Don't Capture Your Intent

    o **Fix**: Emphasize *why* you ask the questions you do. They aren't scripts to memorize; they're expressions of genuine curiosity. If the manager is just parroting your phrases with no real desire to learn from their people, employees will see right through it.

4. **Pitfall**: No Follow-Up "Meta" Sessions

    o **Fix**: Put them on the calendar. If you skip this step, your manager's development stalls. You'll eventually start seeing them making the same mistakes.

5. **Pitfall**: Overcomplicating the Process

    o **Fix**: C.A.S.E. is simple—four questions. Don't bury managers in new acronyms or advanced frameworks. Let them master the basics of question-driven leadership first.

Reality Check: This Is the Future You Signed Up For

Listen, if you're about to scale your business, you can't keep being the wizard behind the curtain for every team problem. So it's time to step into your new role: **mentor of mentors.** The day you see a manager running a perfect C.A.S.E. Method conversation without looking to you for reassurance—that's the day you realize you've multiplied yourself.

But—and here's the subtlety—**you'll never see that day if you keep swooping in to rescue them at every sign of discomfort.** Your managers need space to lead, stumble and grow. Let them fall, let them rise. Let them run C.A.S.E. Method over and over again until they own it. **Your Move: Take the "Manager Shadow" Challenge**

Before you flip to the next chapter, do this:

1. **Pick One Manager** – Write down their name.
2. **Schedule a Shadow Session** – Pick a real task or project they can watch you delegate.
3. **Plan Your Debrief** – Block 15 minutes afterwards to ask them:

   - "Which questions did you see me use that surprised you?"

   - "When did you notice me biting my tongue so the employee could figure it out?"

   - "What's one thing you'd do differently if you were in my seat?"

4. **Co-Lead** – Within two weeks, pick a second task for you and your manager to co-lead using C.A.S.E.
5. **Go Meta** – After that co-lead session, hold a mini C.A.S.E. Method conversation about *their* approach to the C.A.S.E Method.

That's it. Simple, direct, and unstoppable if you stick with it.

If your managers can't replicate your leadership, you're

still the single point of failure. Sure, you may have gained more free time than you had a year ago, but your business can't scale if your managers haven't stepped up to become the real mentors and problem-solvers. This chapter isn't just about giving them a new skill—it's about giving you genuine freedom. The day you walk into the office (or log onto Slack) and see your managers running a crisp C.A.S.E. Method conversation with zero help from you? That's the day you can breathe a sigh of relief… or better yet, book that month-long family trip you've been too busy to take.

Now, let's see just how far we can push this. Ready for the final hand-off?

What if, you could scale your leadership using AI that reflects your style, your voice, and your thinking?

Turn the page—Chapter 10 is going to blow your mind… and clear your calendar. Let's go!

CHAPTER 10 - *LET THE AI TAKE OVER (SO YOU DON'T HAVE TO)*

Imagine a world where every time you teach a task to an employee using the C.A.S.E. Method, an AI "employee assistant" is right there—listening, taking notes, and learning. It retains every question asked and every answer given or organizes all that information so that the next time you need to train someone or refine that process, it can step in for you and guide the discussion. No more being stuck as the bottleneck for your team's growth. No more worrying about things stalling when you're away. Think of the AI as a 24/7 personal trainer for every new and existing staff member.

The End Goal: Removing

Yourself from the Loop

The big shift here is that AI changes the very definition of "manager oversight." Normally, you'd have to be deeply involved in every C.A.S.E. Method cycle whenever a new person joins or a new task arises. They'd come to you for the process, you'd watch them go through it, you'd ask the four questions, you'd revise, and so on—especially when one employee turns around to train another. But now, with AI stepping in, much of that responsibility can shift away from you.

I know how easy it is to say, "Yes, but I'm the only person who fully understands how this is supposed to go." That's exactly the trap we're trying to escape. You don't want your business to grind to a halt whenever you, the owner, are absent. Leveraging an AI assistant that "sits" in on all your C.A.S.E. Method sessions, and learns with each iteration changes this dynamic.

Here's how it might look in practice:

1. **You** (the manager/owner/subject-matter expert) teach the task to an employee for the first time using the C.A.S.E. Method.

2. **The AI assistant** observes, records, and organizes all the Q&A from that session—everything from the big confusions to the tiny clarifications.

3. **Employees** and AI work together for any follow-up cycles. The AI suggests the next round of questions to ask at the "Study" stage based on what's been captured so far.

4. **Manager** gradually steps back, confident that the AI has "seen it all."

5. **Future new hires** learn the same task with the guidance of the AI, referencing all the prior solutions, clarifications, and best practices—without needing the boss to personally re-teach every detail.

Why AI Makes Sense Here

The C.A.S.E. Method hinges on capturing and refining knowledge in a cycle:

- **C (Challenge):** "What challenge did you

have?"

- **A (Articulate):** "What steps did you take?"

- **S (Study):** "Why did you make those choices? Let's dive deeper."

- **E (Easier Than Expected):** "What turned out simpler than you thought?"

Within each step, valuable data emerges—why a decision was made, where confusion crept in, which steps were overly complicated, and so forth. Historically, we'd scribble notes, type them up in a document, and store them someplace. Those notes were often incomplete. People would forget to check them or—worse—lose them.

An AI assistant, on the other hand, captures everything. It can log every bit of conversation, and label each question, each confusion, each correction, each success. It's effectively building a robust reference library—an evolving "playbook" that gets smarter the more your team interacts with it. Then, during the next iteration, the AI can say, "Wait, before we move forward, remember last time you encountered a similar issue at Step 3. Did we address that?" or "Have you considered *this* question? It cleared up confusion before." Suddenly, you're not the only teacher with a perfect memory. The AI does the reminding for you.

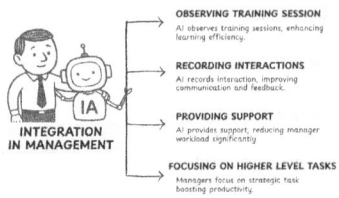

A Quick Story: Passing the Torch, AI Style

Let's say you've got an employee named Robin who's spent months perfecting a particular process—maybe it's setting up email campaigns for your upcoming promotions. You used the C.A.S.E. Method to teach Robin the ropes. You had at least two or three cycles refining the process, fielding her questions, clarifying the tricky parts, and locking down best practices. All of that is stored with the AI assistant.

Now Robin's ready to train the newest hire, Sam. Under normal circumstances, you'd have to be in all of those training sessions—because Robin might know the task, but you're the only one who remembers all the subtle "whys" behind each step. But not anymore. The AI was "in the room" during your sessions with Robin. So, if Sam asks, "Why do we pull open rates first instead of click-through rates?" the AI can step in to say, "Last time, Robin discovered that sorting campaigns by open rates revealed poor deliverability problems first, making the rest of the analysis flow better." This frees Robin from having to recall all the little details from memory and frees you from having to show up at all to confirm the logic. All of the institutional knowledge is baked into the AI's training data—so no single person becomes the bottleneck.

AI-Prompted "Study" Stage

One of the hardest parts of the C.A.S.E. Method is the Study stage because it requires *deep thinking* and reflection:

- **Why** did we do it that way?

- **Were there alternative steps we considered but discarded?

- **Is there some underlying principle at play?

When you rely on purely human memory, it's easy for folks to forget the alternative paths they once considered. With an AI assistant, all those older attempts, plus any questions from earlier cycles, can be recalled instantly. This is where it shines:

- **AI-Prompted Reminders:** "Last time we tried a different route at Step 4. Are we certain we've ruled that out for Sam's scenario?"

- **Expanded Thinking:** "You mentioned confusion about verifying the correct email template. Are we sure we're including the right sign-off? That was an issue a month ago."

- **Error Prevention:** "Historically, the team needed extra checks to ensure compliance. Let's not overlook that again."

Essentially, the AI keeps us honest. It ensures we revisit old mistakes and missed steps, so they don't keep recurring. More importantly, it can proactively ask clarifying questions at the moment *they matter*—not after something has gone wrong and the manager has to swoop in to fix it.

But Won't the AI Get It Wrong?

It's a fair question. Anyone who's ever used a chat-based AI in the real world knows that it can misunderstand, misinterpret, or just flat-out fail. The key to success lies in training the AI *properly* and setting boundaries for when it should take the lead versus when it should kick complicated questions up to a manager. Just like onboarding a new hire, the AI needs a thoughtful introduction to your business operations:

1. **Initial Guidance** – You feed it your core process documentation. Make sure it understands the "happy path" your team typically takes.

2. **Observed Sessions** – The AI "sits in" as you go through multiple C.A.S.E. cycles, so it sees the real friction, real questions, and real answers in context.

3. **Confidence Thresholds** – If it's 80% sure about a suggestion, it can proceed. But if it's lower, it flags a manager. This ensures it doesn't lead employees off a cliff in the name of saving time.

4. **Continuous Feedback Loop** – Your team can "teach" the AI, clarifying, "That answer wasn't correct," or "Actually, we handle that differently now," so the system gets smarter with each iteration.

Yes, there will be some trial and error. But the payoff—freeing yourself from a constant oversight role—is massive.

A Look at the Future

When I say "AI Employee Assistant," I'm talking about a team member with a photographic memory and a keen sense of when to ask a clarifying question. In five or ten years, I can see:

- **Fully Automated Onboarding** – A new staffer can "meet" the AI on Day One and start learning tasks. The system runs them through the basics, quizzes them, checks their performance, and only escalates issues when it detects major confusion or risk.

- **Task-Specific Virtual Mentors** – If you have many different processes, the same AI can morph into slightly different "roles," each specialized in a particular type of task.

- **Auto-Generated Insights** – As the AI sees

repeated confusion around a step, it can prompt you (the owner) to revise the SOP or create an additional resource. It can detect where the biggest knowledge gaps lie—and then propose solutions.

When AI Saves You from Yourself

Bringing AI into the C.A.S.E. Method might feel a bit odd at first—like you're handing your personal "secret sauce" to a piece of software. But let's reframe that. This isn't about replacing your expertise. It's about creating **freedom** for you and **empowerment** for your staff. The AI is simply the tool that accelerates your exit from the day-to-day.

I've always said, "Only I can do this" is a trap. The next-level trap is "Only I can teach this"—that mindset keeps you stuck in the same loop—over and over again With the AI assistant in the room, you're no longer forced to re-hash every nuance, every time. The knowledge is documented, organized, and made continuously available to your team.

Practical Tips to Start AI Integration

Want to begin blending AI into your workflow without overwhelming your team (or yourself)? Start here:

1. **Pick a Pilot Task** – Don't try to AI-enable your entire operation at once. Start with a single process that's well-defined but still has plenty of moving parts. For instance, it might be your blog publishing process or a recurring accounting task—something with clear steps that the AI can easily track.

2. **Record One Entire C.A.S.E. Method Cycle** – Let the AI "observe" the whole session end-to-end, from you handing off the instructions to the employee's attempt, to the final discussion. Label it carefully so you can refer back to it.

3. **Encourage Employees to Ask the AI** – Once that pilot cycle is done, challenge your staff: "Ask the AI first. If you're still stuck, then come to me." This trains them—and the AI—to rely on the knowledge base and refine it further.

4. **Review & Tweak** – Expect to do a few short daily or weekly reviews of how well the AI is performing, where it's misfiring, and how to correct it. By staying on top of it early, you'll avoid big mistakes and get the system tuned faster.

Overcoming The "Comfort" Barrier

One last thing: some leaders get a bit uneasy handing over so much responsibility to technology. That's natural. If you're worried about the AI making a fatal mistake, set guardrails in place. But also remember that your team is *already* missing steps or forgetting small nuances if you're not around. None of us is perfect. With AI, you at least have a **documented, searchable paper trail** showing exactly where things went wrong—and how to fix them. That's far more reliable than relying on memory, sticky notes, or watercooler training.

The beauty of the C.A.S.E. Method is its simplicity:
It captures, refines, and repeats knowledge in a structured loop. And AI thrives on that kind of iteration.

As each day passes, the assistant gets smarter. Your

team gets stronger. And you get freer.

Soon, your employees won't just rely on you to get things done—they'll trust the system. And when that happens, the business can grow without needing *you* in every room.

That's how you truly scale.

Takeaway:

Bringing an AI employee assistant into your C.A.S.E. Method cycles is like giving your team a manager's brain in the room at all times—only this manager doesn't take days off, doesn't forget details, and knows exactly the best moment to ask a clarifying question. The end result? You, the business owner, get the freedom to focus on the bigger-picture strategy or to remove yourself from the day-to-day without worrying that your people will stall out. They've got a new "assistant" to guide them. And over time, the synergy between humans and AI can create processes that are more robust and streamlined than either side could manage alone.

Now, that's real freedom—where every new hire or newly assigned task no longer needs your personal, minute-by-minute input. After all, the ultimate vision of the C.A.S.E. Method was always to make you *unnecessary* for the mechanical parts of the business. Leveraging AI just puts that vision on steroids.

CHAPTER 11 - *I DON'T ANSWER QUESTIONS*

I haven't introduced myself yet. Hi, I'm Atiba. I've been an entrepreneur for over 30 years. I've built and led more than 10 companies across both for-profit and nonprofit spaces. I've formed teams in each one, and I've escaped the "cage" multiple times.

I chose not to introduce myself earlier because this book isn't about me or what the CASE Method has done for my businesses. This book is **all about you**—what the CASE Method can do for *you* and the countless entrepreneurs it's already helped. HOWEVER…

You may have bought this book because you heard me on a podcast or saw me speaking at an event where I said, "I don't answer questions."

If you're a CEO who spends the first few hours of the day fielding question after question from your team, hearing that might sound like a dream come true.

Let me be clear—this isn't about being rude or ignoring your team. It's not arrogance. It's about refusing to become your team's human search engine. When you stop answering every question, you begin to foster a culture of self-sufficiency, creativity, and true ownership.

Sure, it might sound provocative—maybe even like clickbait—but that statement points to something much deeper: a **leadership philosophy** built around **three core principles** that shape everything I do, and everything this book teaches:

1. **Leaders Must Clearly Articulate Vision**
2. **You Can't Build a Thriving Brand Without Great Internal Communication**
3. **Coach Yourself (So You Can Coach Others)**

Let's explore each one, so you can stop being the walking FAQ and start empowering your people to find their own answers.

Principle 1: Leaders Must Clearly Articulate Vision

Andy Stanley, in his book *Visioneering*, defines vision as "a clear mental picture of what could be, fueled by the conviction that it should be." Yet most of us fail to paint that picture in our day-to-day operations. We talk a good game about "mission" and "goals," then completely drop the ball on telling our team—or ourselves—what "success" actually looks like in a given task or project.

Why This Matters

If you can't paint a picture of what "success" means —even for smaller tasks—how can your team make confident decisions? They'll default to you for clarity, firing off endless questions:

- "I wanted to get your approval first."
- "Is this what you want, boss?"
- "Did I do this right?"
- "Are we sure this meets the standard?"

Before you know it, your job is reduced to answering endless questions. You've unknowingly built the cage —and locked yourself inside it.

For most of us, if we're honest, the questions we end up answering are the ones we feel we shouldn't have to. We wonder, "Why don't they know the answer?" or "Why am I explaining this again?" We've all said at some point, "When will they learn to think?" And that's precisely where the C.A.S.E. Method comes in—helping your team think for themselves instead of relying on you for every minor decision.

The Cure: Everyday Vision

You don't need to give a TED Talk for every project. But you *do* need to give a clear, intentional vision. Here's how:

- **Every Project Has a Purpose.** Whether it's sending a proposal or creating a new landing page, define success from the start. For instance: "We want a proposal that leaves zero doubt we understand the client's pain points and have the perfect solution."
- **Every Task Has a Win Condition.** If your employees can't say, "I know exactly what 'great' looks like here," you haven't done your job as a leader.

- **Every Person Needs to Know the 'Why.'** When people grasp the reason behind the vision, they rarely need step-by-step instructions. They can improvise to get the right results.

A Note on Clarity: This step ensures we're communicating effectively and sharing the vision with anyone who'll be responsible for execution. They get to ask questions about the vision upfront—before they start. If they ask a question that's clearly already covered by the vision, I won't answer it. That might sound harsh, but it trains them to rely on the articulated vision.

The 5 W's & 1 H: Quick Handoffs for Simpler Tasks

Not every job warrants a full C.A.S.E. Method deep dive.

Some tasks are simpler, more routine, or have fewer variables. In those cases, I rely on the "5 W's and 1 H" framework: **Who, What, When, Where, Why, and How**.

Incorporating this under Principle 1 keeps the focus on clarity of vision while giving your people a concise roadmap to follow:

1. **Who**

    - Other than the employee being assigned, who else is involved?

2. **What**

    - Clarify the scope. Outline exactly what needs doing—no guesswork.

3. **When**

    - Establish deadlines and milestones. Is this due tomorrow or next week? That drastically changes how someone tackles it.

4. **Where**

    - Identify the location or platform. Are they accessing files on a shared drive? Posting on LinkedIn or the company site?

5. **Why**

    - This is the heartbeat. Explain how this task fits into the bigger picture, why it matters, and who benefits from it. Without this, people lose motivation.

6. **How**

    - Provide guidelines or preferred methods—especially if certain tools or protocols are required.

By handing off simpler tasks with "5 W's + 1 H," you ditch vague one-liners like "Get it done." Instead, you give the precise direction they need—without chaining them to your side. More importantly, you're reminding them that every task relates to the bigger vision—so you're far less likely to get questions on things you've already spelled out.

Principle 2: You Can't Build a Thriving Brand Without Great Internal Communication

A mentor once told me, "Your clients see you the same way your team sees you." That stuck with me. If you're always elusive, perpetually busy, or constantly swooping in at the last minute to "save the day," that chaos seeps into how your brand is perceived—internally and externally.

Why This Matters

Your culture is the bedrock of your brand. We talk about "brand voice," "brand values," and "brand promise"—but guess what shapes those? Internal communication. If your team has to guess what your brand stands for—or worse, tiptoe around your moods and vague expectations—that confusion eventually shows up in your customer experience. It becomes baked into your systems, your service, and your storytelling. A strong external brand starts with clarity and trust *inside* your company walls.

The Cure: Intentional Communication

- Starts with values.

What are the values your company lives by? Not the ones you say are your core values that no one knows. What values are you actually living day in and day out? Every business has values, and either they are set and instilled by you or they are set and instilled by your staff. Someone is in control, and if you are not confident it's you, it's them. Now that could be a good thing, AND it could be bad. Bottom line: if values are not instilled from the top down, you will never achieve sustainability. You must identify the values, personally live the values, and celebrate when team members live the values too.

- **Don't Just "Talk at" People—Engage Them.**

We all hate meetings. We have too many, and often they are just complaint fests or wastes of time. Each department of our company has team meetings. All of our team meetings start with discussing Personal Wins. These are outside-of-work things that employees are excited about. We then move into professional wins. Often, there are KPI reports and status updates that follow, and we end by discussing Challenges and where we need courage for the upcoming week.

Remember, it's all about the questions you ask. We get the same data you do in your company meetings, but ours leaves staff members feeling cared for, heard, and even empowered. Creating a safe space for people to share where they need courage in the upcoming week is powerful. It helps each of us think about our roles differently, be vulnerable, and allow others to share insights and support.

- **Admit When You're Vague.**

Sometimes I find myself tossing out half-ideas. One of the truths of leadership in business is that we often have to make decisions and set direction with only 1/3 of the information we would like available. When I'm unsure...I admit it. Getting back to the points above about courage...we need courage too...when we do, I show up and say it. Then I open the floor and ask this: "What's on your mind about this?" I don't ask what do you think, or do you have any questions....those questions illicit the same reactions we have to that annoying guy in the middle of the mall selling skin care...we just say "no".

When you build a culture rooted in clear, honest, two-way communication, your team doesn't need to run everything by you. They *think*, they *decide*, and they come back with *solutions*, not questions.

That's how you grow a brand from the inside out. Your team becomes so aligned with the vision and values that they naturally evolve into confident, mission-driven ambassadors, without needing constant direction.

Principle 3: Coach Yourself

My son's QB coach, Bryson Spinner, had a rule he drilled into every player on Day 1: "You must learn to coach yourself." Why? Because once the ball is snapped, the coach can't come onto the field to rescue you. He can't tell you between plays that your last throw sailed because you used a #1 arm angle instead of #2. The QB must assess himself—right there on the field—against the "vision" of what was supposed to happen and what happened and correct it. It's the same way in business: when employees are in the middle of a crisis, they can't just holler for you to run on and fix everything. In that moment, they need to make smart decisions on their own.

Why This Matters

If your team never learns to be self-sufficient under pressure, you'll always be the one to bail them out. You might preach about vision and culture, but the minute a challenge appears, they run to you. They must learn, you must teach them to coach themselves.

The Cure: Ownership Mindset

- **Pinpoint the Bottleneck**: Theory of Constraints teaches that in any system or process, one constraint—one "weakest link"—ultimately determines how fast or effectively everything else can move. Essentially, it pinpoints root cause issues. Helping your staff learn how to find the root causes of issues gives them an invaluable tool in their process of taking ownership. If your team can't see the true bottleneck, they'll spin their wheels or throw random guesses at the problem, never resolving the real issue. TOC helps them drill down to the root cause, so they can apply the right fix and move on confidently.

- **Give People the Tools for Self-Coaching.** Show them frameworks—like the C.A.S.E. Method—that they can rely on when you're not around. Let them become their own resource. Yes, an employee can use the CASE Method questions on themselves and this only works when they can clearly identify the goal and the problem.

- **Hold Them to Game-Time Standards.** Just like a quarterback can't wait until halftime to figure out where they messed up, your employees shouldn't wait for your post-mortem. They need to make in-the-moment calls. When the pressure hits, they think, "What's the vision here? How do I course-correct?"—instead of shouting, "Boss, help!"

By instilling this "coach yourself" mindset, you free your team to act without relying on you for every tiny decision. Instead of calling you in for a rescue, they adapt on the fly—making informed, vision-aligned choices in real time. That's how you end up with real players, not passive spectators.

Tying It All Together

Do I literally never answer questions? Of course not. I'd

be a terrible leader if I withheld critical information. But I do make a habit of pushing questions back onto the asker. If someone says, "How should I handle this?" I respond, "How do you think it should be handled?"

Yes, it can be maddening for an employee at first. But here's what happens: they articulate their reasoning, obstacles, and how they interpret your vision. Suddenly, they see the answer on their own. In five minutes, they've grown more than if you'd given them a one-line directive.

That's a far better gift than a quick fix.

Final Word

This entire book—and the whole C.A.S.E. Method—rests on the principle that your business should run on systems and thinking that no longer have to come from you. That only happens if you force clarity upfront (articulate the vision), build unstoppable internal communication, and empower everyone to coach themselves first.

So the next time a team member corners you with, "Hey, can you tell me how to—" try responding, "Walk me through your thought process first." Watch them pause. Watch them think. And then—watch them grow.

Do that consistently for the next 18 months, and here's what you'll see:

You're no longer the bottleneck.

Your brand, your people, your culture—they're thriving, independently.

And you? You've stepped into true leadership.

That, my friend, is the dream.

It begins the moment you stop answering every question—and start leading with clarity, communication, and a culture of self-coaching.

CHAPTER 12 - *ORIGINS OF THE C.A.S.E. METHOD*

SEO research is about as riveting as watching paint dry. Most entrepreneurs either outsource it or cross their fingers and hope for the best. I ran a marketing agency that had specialized in SEO since 1996—literally before the term was invented. For me, picking winning keywords was second nature. I could glance at a list of 2,000 phrases and instantly spot the top 10 that would rank on Page 1 of Google in 60 days.

By 2021 it was time for me to step back from doing SEO myself (It took me a while to let go, that's why I know how you feel). I hired Kristine. Her one job: *"Learn how my brain works."* That's what I told her—on her very first day. Her first few months were awful.

Kristine had come from a different background. She'd picked up black-hat SEO tricks in her previous job. And to make things more complicated, we weren't just doing traditional SEO—we were doing video SEO, trying to rank YouTube videos on Google. At the time, in 2021, there were no clear guides, blogs, or tutorials for this. The method we were using? I had developed it myself. And Kristine just wasn't getting it.

Almost every meeting ended with her in tears or wanting to quit, and me talking her off the ledge. Kristine was young and smart, so I knew she could and would get it...just could not figure out why she wasn't. I couldn't understand why she could not see what was so obviously obvious to me in the research.

One Tuesday morning—our usual meeting day—I said to myself, *"Atiba, we can't make this young lady cry again today."*

I knew I had to do something different.

I wasn't sure what exactly, but I knew one thing: *Don't ask the same questions you've been asking every week.*

So instead of starting with, *"What did you do this week?"* or *"What went wrong?"*—I simply asked:

"Hey Kristine, what was challenging for you this week?"

That one question changed everything.

For the first time, I wasn't focused on critiquing her actions—I was listening to how she *thought*. She opened up about her challenges and the things that led to success and failure. I heard what she was trying to solve, not just what she got wrong. I began to understand *how* she viewed the work.

And for the first time, I realized something important:

She didn't need more instruction—she needed connection.

THE DELEGATION TRAP

What You Ask Shapes What You Hear

By shifting the conversation away from fault-finding and toward curiosity, I finally got to hear her thought process. I saw, clearly, the difference between how *she* saw the world and how *I* did. And that opened the door to actually coaching her—instead of just correcting her.

Instinctively, after sharing her challenges, she wanted to know if I wanted to know the steps she took. Right there was born question #2 of the CASE Method.

After she walked me through the steps she had taken, we spent the rest of the hour discussing just a few of them. An old mentor of mine, JR Ridinger, taught me that "the mind can only absorb what the rear end can endure". That stuck with me. It's how I learned that four steps were the ideal number to cover with our team during any session. Anything more, and people start to zone out.

Weeks later—during either our 4th or 5th iteration weeks—we had a little extra time in our meeting, and I asked her something different.

Now that you are starting to get the hang of this, what turned out to be easier than you expected? Her answer shocked me—and gave birth to the fourth question of the C.A.S.E Method.

In one of the areas, Kristine said she found easy, we were able to see a hidden talent that she had for SEO research—something *I* didn't even possess. That moment showed me the real value of asking better questions: not just to teach, but to reveal genius.

Realizing We Had a System

Two years later, a fellow CEO asked me how I could travel so much without my company grinding to a halt. *"My team freezes whenever I'm out of the office,"* she said. *"I can't imagine them doing high-level work if I'm not there holding their hand."*

That's when it hit me: the only difference between her team and mine was that my team had learned how to think independently. And it all started with a few, deceptively simple questions.

I had unknowingly created a method to transfer my "CEO brain" into others. That method allowed me to step away without the company grinding to a halt.

Over time, we slapped a label on it—The C.A.S.E. Method—and started formalizing how we used it. But it all started with Kristine, a frustrated SEO researcher who just needed me to get out of my own head and walk her through the logic behind what I did.

My "Smartest Guy In The Room" Trap

Before that breakthrough with Kristine, I was the guy who'd burned his last company to the ground, convinced I had no other choice. I wanted a culture of ownership, but I was still the biggest bottleneck. It never occurred to me that my team didn't just need steps—they needed my thought process. They needed me to ask questions that teased out their own expertise.

Once I saw that, I couldn't unsee it. From that point on, whenever I hired someone, I made one thing clear: *I'm not going to answer every question. I'm going to show you how to solve it yourself.* And guess what? People rose to that challenge. Some left because they wanted hand-holding. But the ones who stayed thrived.

CHAPTER 13 - *MY MISSION*

Why I Believe This Is The Last Book On Employee Productivity You'll Ever Need

I began this book with a bold prediction: this could be the last nonfiction business book on employee productivity you'll ever need.

That might sound arrogant—maybe even unrealistic. After all, countless productivity and management books flood bookstores every year. So why do I stand by that statement?

Because nearly every "employee productivity" solution I've come across treats only the *symptoms* of underperformance—offering surface-level tips, trendy tools, and time-management hacks—while ignoring the root cause: **you**, the founder or leader, and how you teach your people to think.

As long as you believe you must be involved in every decision, showing up like a crisis-fighting superhero, you'll stay trapped in a cycle of overwork, burnout, and untapped potential.

The C.A.S.E. Method flips that script. Instead of giving you yet another list of tasks or so-called best practices, it shows you how to *transfer your genius*—your thinking, your decision-making prowess—to your team. It puts you on the path to building a culture where employees solve problems, meet challenges, and even *fail forward* without your constant intervention.

I'm not saying there aren't other great books on leadership or productivity out there—of course, there are. But once you learn to make your team think like owners (not order-takers), you'll find you have far less need to wade through every new management theory.

You'll have already built a system where your people's *own* creativity and thinking lift your company to new heights. That's why I can say—confidently and without hesitation—that this may truly be the *last* productivity book you'll ever need.

We've Been Taught to Lead the Wrong Way

Most of us grew up watching leaders who seemed larger than life—constantly barking orders, slicing through daily fires, and making snap decisions. Their teams? Left to play "follow the boss." Over time, we internalized that "good leadership" equals doing the heavy lifting ourselves, saving the day at the last minute, and pulling 60-hour weeks while the rest of the staff depends on us for every major call.

The tragedy of that style is twofold:

1. **It buries your team's potential.** If employees never

get to *practice* owning decisions, they never develop the confidence and skill to excel.

2. **It buries *you*.** Doing everything yourself leaves you exhausted. You become the limiting factor to your own business's growth.

That's the old model. And if you've made it this far, you're probably ready to leave it behind.

My Mission: 1 Million Business Owners Using the C.A.S.E. Method

Why did I write this book? Simple:

My personal mission is to help 1 million business owners worldwide learn and adopt the C.A.S.E. Method—because I've seen firsthand how it transforms not just a business, but a leader's entire life. You and I are the bedrock of the world's economy and society. It's not big business or government… It's us. When we are better leaders, the world will also be a better place to live for all.

THE DELEGATION TRAP

The End of Hero Leadership and
the Start of Ownership Culture

Over the past years, I've shared this method at workshops, on podcasts, in mastermind groups, and through keynotes for entrepreneurial communities. I've watched:

- **Burned-out CEOs** finally take real vacations—returning to find their companies running smoothly without them.

- **Overworked managers** discover they *love* mentoring a junior staffer who's eager to learn how to "think like the boss."

- **Young employees** blossom into star performers because, for the first time, their creativity and decision-making are *trusted* and *developed*, not micromanaged.

Seeing these transformations solidified what I want for my life's work. Entrepreneurs are the ones who solve the world's biggest problems—so imagine the ripple effect of *liberating* them from the Founder's Trap, letting them scale their visions far beyond a single person's bandwidth.

It Starts With You—But You Can't Do It Alone

Yes, you're reading this book, probably feeling a surge of excitement at the prospect of truly offloading your critical tasks without forfeiting quality. But excitement alone doesn't guarantee success. You'll need:

1. **Personal Commitment:** *You* have to decide you won't default to old habits. No more "I'll do it myself—it's faster."

2. **An Accountability Triad:** As you learned in Chapter 4, surrounding yourself with two other driven entrepreneurs or leaders who challenge and support you is a game-changer. Let them hold you accountable when you slip into micromanagement or "superhero mode."

3. **A Willing Team (or at Least One Willing Person):** You don't need your entire staff on board from day one—just find the right individual who's hungry to learn and grow. Success with that one delegated task can serve as proof that the C.A.S.E. Method works in your environment.

Once the momentum starts rolling, your team will see

the difference in how *they* get to grow. They'll realize you trust them *and* you're giving them the framework to succeed. That's a powerful combination.

I Want to Hear Your Stories

One of my greatest joys these days is hearing directly from entrepreneurs who've taken the plunge, used the C.A.S.E. Method, and seen their businesses (and personal lives) transformed. Maybe you:

- Delegated a high-stakes client project for the first time in years—only to discover your team came up with a more creative strategy than you expected.

- Reduced your weekly hours from 70 to 35 because your employees are now self-sufficient and *love* learning how to think, not just do.

- Spotted new opportunities for growth

because you finally had the mental bandwidth to plan, strategize, or just *breathe*.

Whatever your story, I'd love to hear it. Visit *CasemethodBook.com/EscapeTheCage* and share how your own "escape from the cage" is going. Who knows—your journey might inspire another burned-out founder to finally see that letting go is possible.

What Comes Next

I'll let you in on a secret: the C.A.S.E. Method is not the "final" system you'll ever create. It's simply the foundation. Over time, you'll probably adapt it, fold in advanced tools, or even build your own frameworks that layer on top of these four questions. *That's the point.* Once your people learn how to analyze challenges, articulate steps, study decisions, and celebrate what was easier than expected, you're already in a perpetual cycle of innovation.

The big difference is that *none* of those ongoing improvements will rely on you personally. Your team will refine the method themselves—and pass it on to new hires. Your managers will become mentors to the next wave of leaders. And eventually, as we discussed in Chapter 10, AI co-pilots could handle the daily grunt work of guiding employees through known pitfalls, letting you focus on strategy or even that side passion you've been ignoring for years.

All because you decided to let go of the illusion that only *you* can do (or teach) the work at hand.

My Final Ask

If you've gleaned value here, do two things:

1. **Implement the C.A.S.E. Method** on at least one critical, high-impact task within the next seven days. Don't wait. Don't say "later." Pick that first "only I can do this" project and jump in.

2. **Spread the Word** to someone else. Another founder, CEO, or team leader who's drowning in daily tasks. Let them know there *is* a better way—and that you've already started.

We can't change old leadership habits overnight, but one by one, we can model a new standard—one where delegation isn't a dreaded chore, but an opportunity to help others *think* and *excel*.

That's my mission: **To help 1 million business owners worldwide adopt the C.A.S.E. Method** so they can build the thriving, sustainable companies they once dreamed of—without burning out or giving up the high standards that set them apart in the first place.

If you're still reading, you're part of that mission.
And I'm grateful you're here.

Now go. Show the world what your team can do—when they don't have to wait for you to make every decision.

—Atiba

P.S. I genuinely want to hear from you. Visit my website TheDelegationTrap.com/MeetAtiba. Tell me how the C.A.S.E. Method is changing your day-to-day operations—or share the biggest challenges you still face. Let's keep building this revolution together.

REFERENCES & FURTHER READING

• Harvard Business Review (2024): *"Why Teams that Fail Productively Outperform Teams that Strive for Perfection,"* Harvard Business Review, Vol. 102.

• Stanford Graduate School of Business (2022): *"Adaptive Leadership and the Role of Constructive Failure,"* Journal of Organizational Research.

• MIT Sloan (2023): *"The Innovation Edge: How Mini-Failures Drive Breakthroughs,"* MIT Sloan Management Review.

• Brené Brown (2025): *Leading with Vulnerability: How Honest Leaders Transform Teams.*

• Gallup (2023): *"Employee Engagement Decline: The High Cost of Zero-Tolerance Cultures,"* Gallup Workplace Report.

- Deloitte (2024): *"Delegation, Decision-Making, and the Path to Sustainable Growth,"* Deloitte Insights.

- Change Your Questions, Change Your Life by Marilee Adams (Referenced in Chapter 7).

- Atomic Habits by James Clear (for general references on habit-building and iteration).

- Winston Churchill's Quote: *"Success is stumbling from failure to failure with no loss of enthusiasm."*

ACKNOWLEDGEMENTS

To my exceptional team: Throughout my career, I've had the privilege of building many successful teams, but none have performed with your extraordinary caliber. When I embarked on creating an international team centered in the Philippines, skeptics warned, "You'll be trapped—Filipinos are great workers but not strategic thinkers." You've shattered those misconceptions completely. It's because of your brilliance that we developed the C.A.S.E. Method. It's because of your dedication that I've found the freedom to truly serve as CEO. My deepest gratitude to each of you.

Family forms the foundation of all achievement. Tanika, my wife, you witnessed my leadership journey from its rockiest moments—hiring over a hundred people in a single year to fill just six positions, and then repeating that process the following year. You stood beside me when I was a flawed leader, supporting me in countless ways that words cannot adequately express. And to my children, who have taught me more about authentic leadership and humanity than anyone else in this world—thank you for making me better every day.

Kasim Aslam and Kyle McGlotten, your impact has been transformative. Kyle, over a decade ago, you recognized something in me that I couldn't yet see, insisting that people needed to hear my voice. When I wasn't ready—when I faltered and nearly surrendered—Kasim appeared as the catalyst I needed. Kasim, you truly saw me, reinforcing Kyle's earlier insight that I had valuable wisdom to share and a responsibility to voice it.

I would be remiss not to acknowledge Christina Hooper and Michael DeLon. For years, you both insisted I needed to write this book while I stubbornly resisted. Your persistence and unwavering presence finally broke through my reluctance, and for that, I am profoundly grateful.

Made in the USA
Coppell, TX
24 February 2026